Commentary on the Book
Over the Storms of Life

Over the Storms of Life is a book worth reading. J.O.Y Aladetan writes from a pastoral point of view. A storms may come unannounced – how can you deal with that difficult situation? To get the most from the storms of life, I suggest you read the entire book for a better understanding. I strongly recommend this book to scholars and pastors alike, to awaken their minds to the reality of difficult situations and how you can overcome those obstacles ahead of you with the help of God. This book will give you guidance when you go through trials, persecutions, punishment, and afflictions, and it will highlight the differences between these situations.

'God is not a man that He should lie, nor a son of man that he should repent' (Num. 23:19). The vision is for an appointed time, and it will surely manifest

Dr Isaac Ojutalayo
DMin, DD, MA, BS, BATh

The human journey on planet Earth is full of earthly vagaries that sometimes bother one and tend to shake the faith of believers. This book addresses in detail the essence of these vagaries and provides answers to the following questions:

- Why do we pass through the storms of life?
- What is the essence of the storms?
- How do we pass through the storms?
- What are the benefits of passing through successfully?
- What happens if we fail to pass through successfully?
- How do we retrace our steps to come back if we have once failed?

This book gives a balanced and practical view of earthly storms, noting the significance of a sound foundation in the Christian faith and the importance of moving only in accordance to God's will. No one drives himself and overcomes earthly storms. Hence Paul said in Phil 4 that "I can do all things through Christ who strengthens me." If God be for me, who or what storms of life can overpower me?

I find the book relevant for present-day Christians who are battling with all forms of storms. It serves as a useful guide and reference material to assist us all and remind us that whatever situation we may be passing through, it is for a short time. It will soon vanish if we only remain in the Lord and in absolute obedience to His commands.

I commend the initiative of the writer and recommend the book as good material for all Christians, both now and in the future. Explore it and be stronger to sail through earthly vices and satanic attacks. Remain blessed as you read. I pray that God will visit all readers of the book to silence all earthly storms for a lifetime of peace in God's vineyard. In Jesus's mighty name – amen.

Mrs Toyin Oluitan, PhD
Pastor and Lecturer

This book is a 'Peace, be still' voice of the Lord to anyone who needs an understanding of why and how to surf the storms of life, be these professional, marital, parental, financial, physical, or spiritual challenges in their lives. In the words of the author, some promises may take years or decades to manifest. Some may be fast, while some may even take you to the valley of death. Rest assured of His presence to see you through and establish His greatness in you. He is God, who can do all things for those who believe and trust Him.

I recommend this book as a tool of empowerment for those who are comforted and for those who need to be comforted whilst faithfully standing firm and trusting in His Word and covenant promises.

Pastor Mary Macaulay
London

God is not a man that He should lie, nor a son of man that he should repent.

Numbers 23:19

OVER THE STORMS OF *Life*

God's Word and Covenant Promises Prevails

J. O. Y ALADETAN

Copyright © 2019 by Y.O. Aladetan All Rights Reserved.

No part of this publication may be reproduced, distributed, or transmitted in any form or by any means, including photocopying, recording, or other electronic or mechanical methods, without the prior written permission of the author, except in the case of brief quotations embodied in critical reviews and certain other noncommercial uses permitted by copyright law. For permission requests, write to the author via the publisher, addressed "Attention: Permissions Coordinator," at the address below.

ARPress
45 Dan Road Suite 36
Canton MA 02021

Hotline: 1(800) 220-7660
Fax: 1(855) 752-6001

Ordering Information:
Quantity sales. Special discounts are available on quantity purchases by corporations, associations, and others. For details, contact the publisher at the address above.

Printed in the United States of America.

ISBN-13:	Softcover	979-8-89389-400-4
	Hardcover	979-8-89389-402-8
	eBook	979-8-89389-401-1

Library of Congress Control Number: 2024916603

I dedicate this book to Jehovah, almighty God, the Creator of heaven and the earth; to Jesus Christ, the Son of God and the Redeemer of the world; and to the Holy Spirit, the abiding God who dwells in man to comfort, guide, heal, teach, and lead believers into righteousness.

To all the ambassadors and disciples of Jesus Christ worldwide, you're the apparent heirs to the kingdom of God.

I further dedicate this book to my teacher, Pastor G. O. Baptist, the president of Equipping the Saints Africa and UK Mission, who agreed to write a foreword for this book but quietly went to rest in the Lord less than twenty hours after his agreement with me. May his soul rest in peace.

Also, this book is dedicated to my parents, who laid my footsteps on the path of the cross, and to my family, for their unwavering support.

CONTENTS

Foreword xi
Preface xiii
Acknowledgements xvii
Author's Prayer xix
Introduction xxi

Chapter 1   In the Beginning 1
Chapter 2   The Genesis of Promises 26
Chapter 3   Joseph's Dream Promise 65
Chapter 4   Davidic Covenant 94
Chapter 5   God's Manifold Promises 137
Chapter 6   Beyond the Natural 195
Chapter 7   The End Time 213

Conclusion 261
Hymn for the Book 263
About the Author 265
About the Book 267

FOREWORD

I count it a great honour to be asked to write the foreword for this inspiring book.

I am excited and proud of Evangelist Joseph O. Y Aladetan. He writes as he ministers: with power and passion for the Word. When you read this book as carefully as I read the manuscript, you simply won't put it down easily. It will open your inner eyes to the foundation of some of your long-term problems and offer you divine solutions.

Life is a roller coaster, full of ups and downs; however, we thank God for giving us the Prince of Peace, who will always arrest the storms in our lives when we call on Him. This book identifies the principles of God that must be adhered to by Christians in order to defeat the Devil, who is the author and the sole originator of the storms of life.

Jesus Christ, the Master, gave the assurance that we should cheer up as we take our share in the tribulations of life because He has conquered the world on our behalf. As an act of wisdom, if we want to be champions in this world, we must make Jesus our Lord and Commander in our personal struggles and allow Him to be in the forefront of our lives.

Storms of life are inevitable as long as we are in this world. Since Satan lost his position in heaven and fell to the world with some of the host of heaven as his demons, everyone is challenged at one time or the other with afflictions, temptations, and trials of faith.

As you read this book, you will discover that even Christians are not exempted from the battles of life. Paul the apostle encouraged us to endure hardship as good soldiers of Christ. Therefore, be strong in the grace that is in Christ Jesus. Every Christian is fighting some form of battle. Consequently, we are to be sober and vigilant. Our Adversary is as a roaring lion, walking about, seeking whom he may devour (1 Pet. 5:8).

The nature of the battle is spiritual. We must be spiritually inclined so as not to be defeated.

Finally, my brethren, be strong in the Lord and in the power of His might. Put on the whole armour of God, which is Jesus Christ, that you may be able to stand against the wiles of the Devil (Eph. 6:11).

Whoever seeks to know the truth will find this book quite enlightening about how to weather the storms of life. Evangelist Aladetan has without doubt clarified and established the importance of aligning with God on our journey. He has analysed case studies of many characters in the Bible who passed through the storms of life, showing us how they became either victors or victims of their circumstances.

The experiences shared in this book are compelling and useful for us in finding solutions to whatever we may be passing through.

I have known Evangelist Joseph O. Y Aladetan to be a true servant of God. He has put many years of research and practical life experiences into this book.

Be blessed mightily as you read.

Pastor Felix O. Makanjuola
Redeemed Christian Church of God
National Coordinator UK School of Disciples

PREFACE

This book is intended to build a dynamic, living faith in the hearts of readers and believers; to create a powerful understanding; and to strengthen them while facing challenges in moments of affliction.

For some people, the way to their palace is through enslavement and imprisonment, like Joseph. For others, the way to their greatness and breakthrough is in the gate and persecution, like Mordekhai. Some find their way to prime ministership through the den of the lion, like Daniel. Others endure the furnace, like Shedrack, Meshach, and Abednego.

Some may find the way to their royal thrones via confinement to the shepherd bush, like David. For many others, the way to the Promised Land is by means of enslavement, like the Israelites. Some secure an everlasting covenant for their generation by means of an act of giving, such as the unusual sacrificial offering of Abraham, because no seed can multiply by itself. It must be planted, die, germinate, and then grow to produce multiple seeds.

For some, the way to give birth to glorious children is to be barren, like Sarah, Rachael, Hannah, and Elizabeth. For others, the road to manifold restoration is to lose all things, like Job.

For a few, the way to supernatural breakthrough is to be rejected and crucified like Jesus Christ, the Son of God.

Ultimately, this book is meant to enlighten readers about God's unfailing love, trustworthiness, and faithfulness. He will never, ever fail nor forsake His children amid the storms. He will always make

Trust in the Word and Promises of God

way where there is no way, so that enemies may know that they are limited and that God is omnipotent and unlimited.

Sadly, many of us focus on the Devil and other enemies while going through trial, without considering the trial of faith from God. The Bible says, 'If God is with us, who can be against us?' (Rom, 28:31). If things are working against you as you bear the promises of God, then God must be involved, as He was with Joseph, David, Jeremiah, and Jesus Christ. The Bible says, 'See, I have refined you, though not as silver, I have tested you in the furnace of affliction' (Isa. 48:10).

The Bible also says, 'Behold, I am the Lord, the God of all flesh: is there anything too hard for me?' (Jer. 32:27).

Two voices speak differently into human lives. First is the voice of God, speaking words of blessing, fruitfulness, multiplication, and peace from Genesis 1:28 through God's anointed men and women. Second is the voice of the Devil, speaking evil words of doom, destruction, and death through satanic prophets to bring about storms (John 10:10). Whose words are you believing and appropriating into your life? You are whom you are because of your belief.

God spoke His Word in the beginning to bring light over the darkness that covered the deep, and the light brought illumination to disperse darkness (Gen. 1:1–4).

God spoke His Word through Moses over the Red Sea, and the sea parted for the Israelites to walk on dry land (Exod. 14).

Jesus spoke over Lazarus who was dead and buried, and Lazarus rose from the grave (John 11:38–44).

Jesus commanded the storms to stop, and it stopped (Mark 4:35–41).

Jesus healed all manners of sickness and disease by the power of His word (Matt. 4:23–24).

Jesus said, 'Verily, verily I say unto you. He that believeth on me, the works that I do he will do also, and greater works than these shall he do because I go unto my Father' (John 14:12).

No one is called gold without going through the fire. Believe and appropriate the words of life into your circumstances.

ACKNOWLEDGEMENTS

I thank those who rendered help to me during the preparation of this book. I thank all of my colleagues, pastors, friends, and family members worldwide for their moral and spiritual support for the success of this writing. I commend the advice and the encouragement of apostle and pastor Dr Oluitan. I remember the kindness of Mrs Dola Falola and her children, and the love they showed to me when God ordered my steps to the United Kingdom.

Pastor Kolawole Akindiya and Elder Charles Banji Fasoranti: thanks for your unconditional love.

To my editorial team, Pastor Yemi Olumodeji, Pastor Funke I. Alliu, and Sister Olagbende K. Onile-ere: well done.

The loving support of my family cannot be overemphasised. I salute you all.

AUTHOR'S PRAYER

My heavenly Father, Your kingdom is eternal, full of love, truth, joy, peace, blessings, and prosperity. Let Your kingdom be established in the hearts of readers of this book. Let them be established in Your kingdom to enjoy ever-flowing mercy, favour, glory, and grace, and Your presence forever. I pray that they be established as an eternal glory. The little among them shall become an eternal glory and powerful nations.

Father Lord, remember all the promises which You have made to them from eternity past, and hasten their fulfilment by Your Spirit. Father Lord, I pray that the Devil will not steal the reader of this book from your kingdom, and that their blessings will abide forever. Father Lord, let my prayer for the readers of my book be my portion and that of my future generations. In Jesus's name, amen.

INTRODUCTION

On my arrival in the UK, when God ordered my footsteps there many years ago, my immediate priority was to take a month's rest before engaging myself to do anything. As I lay on the bed in the room provided for me by the Falolas in south-east London, I began to meditate on the love of God for mankind and what I needed to do to impact lives as a minister of God.

I picked up my pen to write a few lines to explain the irrevocable love of God for mankind, with the aim of printing some tracts for distribution. Then the Holy Spirit flashed my heart to behold the heart of Jesus Christ on the cross at Calvary, filled with undying love for the entire human race.

I was moved further to write on what was revealed to me. It was quite amazing and very interesting that my proposed one-month resting period was what I used to write almost half of my book *The Ninth Hour Miracle: Victory of the Cross* and to conceive the idea of this book, *Over the Storms of Life*.

I went into a deep meditation over the irrevocable promises of God and also considered the faithfulness of God in all His promises throughout the pages of the Scripture, from one generation to another, consequential to the gift of His only begotten Son, our Lord Jesus Christ, the Lamb of God who was crucified on the cross at Calvary to redeem the world.

I was motivated and challenged by this revelation of truth to write on this subject, to activate the giant faith inside every believer's heart. The Bible says, 'Now faith is being sure of what we hope for and certain of what we do not see. This is what the ancients were commended for' (Heb. 11:1–2).

Specifically, this book will remind readers that the promises of God for faithful believers are irrevocable. Fulfilment may be quick or prolonged. Some promises may lead the beneficiary into the furnace of affliction, like those of Abraham, Joseph, and David, before fulfilment.

If God has filled your life with His glory and prepared a place for you in His kingdom, the Devil will try to rob you and take you through a furnace of afflictions. He will wage war against you and battle with you because his ministry is to steal, kill, and destroy. The Devil will try to lead you into difficult challenges, and God may allow it as a process of refinement.

Don't be apprehensive. Don't give up the battle. Maintain your faith like Abraham, Joseph, Job, and David. God is with you in the battle. Your affliction is to prepare you for greater challenges in the work of the kingdom of God. The Bible says, 'See, I have refined you, thou not as silver; I have tested you in the furnace of affliction' (Isa. 48:10).

The Lord promises to refine and purify us by allowing us to go through difficult challenges. This process prepares us to inherit the blessings God has in store for us. The furnace of affliction can be very painful and tough, but the rewards are very pleasant.

You may be tempted to query God because of these experiences. You may wonder why God would call you with promises and yet allow you to face such painful challenges. In the same way that life's preparation begins with elementary school and goes on to university, so also God prepares His own for the works of the ministry. The Bible says, 'And the God of all grace who called you in His eternal glory in Christ, after you have suffered a little while, will Himself restore you and make you strong, firm and steadfast' (1 Pet. 5:10).

God's way of doing things is to give us the test, stay at our sides as we go through the ordeal, and gently embrace us, asking, 'What have you learned from this experience?' Thus, with God our learning grows out of our testing.

For instance, Noah was called when he was aged 500 to prepare to build the ark, but the manifestation of the flood did not take place until he was 600 years old – one hundred years of preparation, mockery, and toiling. Abraham was called when he was 75 years old, but his promises did not manifest until he was 100 – twenty-five years of preparation.

Joseph had his own calling at the age of 17, but did not achieve his place until the age of 30. He was led through thirteen years in the furnace of affliction, from cistern to slavery to prison and finally to the palace, in order to have his promises fulfilled. Moses was called at the age of 40, but he was not sent until the age of 80. Joshua also spent forty years preparing under Moses before his ministry actually began.

David was called at a tender age of 17 to be king over Israel but did not ascend the throne until he became 33 years old – sixteen years of preparation through wars and persecutions. Jesus spent thirty years to prepare for three and a half years of ministry. Paul spent fourteen years in the wilderness on his own preparation.

There is always a difference between the time of calling and the time of sending. This is referred to as the period of preparation. No man is recruited by a nation to be a soldier without military training to make him fit for battle. The same is applicable to the elect of God. The Bible says, 'As the rain and the snow come down from heaven, and do not return to it without watering the earth and making it bud and flourish, so that it yields seed for the sower and bread for the eater, so is my word that goes out from my mouth; It will not return to me empty, but will accomplish what I desire and achieve the purpose for which I sent it' (Isa. 55:10–11 NIV).

God has His own way of taking His elect through the process of refinement, to be made fit for the work of the kingdom and to finish well. The pattern of trials for each of the elect varies, but the good news is that God will never forsake His own. Neither will He allow the rods of the wicked to fall on them.

I am quite sure that you're saying in your heart that you are not called because you're not an apostle, prophet, evangelist, pastor, teacher, reverend, or bishop. I want you to know that everyone created by God is created to live and be a blessing to others. You are called. The Bible says, 'Many are the affliction of the righteous, but the Lord delivered him out of them all. He keepeth all his bones not one of them is broken' (Ps. 34:19–20).

In the lives of His elect, God is ever present to protect and to fight every battle of their lives. He gives believers victory each time they are going through the furnace of affliction. You are crushed for a purpose, and to be a testimony for other so that God can be glorified on earth. You are a true representative of God; hence you were created in His image and likeness. The Bible says, 'When you pass through the waters, I will be with you and when you pass through the rivers, they will not sweep over you. When you walk through the fire, you will not be burned; the flames will not set you ablaze' (Isa. 43:2)

After all, the Devil is not prepared to wage war with empty vessels. The reason he is attacking you is because you are the bearer of God's promises. You are the co-heir to the blessings of Abraham and have a place in the kingdom of God. There is a substance in you which is the Glory of God; hence the attack is intended to steal, kill, or destroy what God has given you. Satan did same to Adam and Eve in the garden of Eden.

You must faithfully fight back by standing firm and trusting in His Word and covenant promises. Every promise of God demands our trust, obedience, and faithfulness in Him who promised. God guarantees our victory in every battle. The Bible says, 'God is not a man, that He should lie nor a son of man, that He should repent. Has He said, and will He not do it? Or has He spoken, and will He not make it good?' (Num. 23:19).

You are crushed for a purpose. You can be a testimony and a solution for someone. God wants to take all the glory at the hilltop of your challenges, giving proof to your adversaries that He is the omnipotent God, the Mighty One in battle, who can do all things. Don't give up before the manifestation of your miracle. Stand up, cheer up, and stay focused.

This book will remind believers that some promises may take a while to manifest. Some may even take you to the valley of death, like Daniel, Shedrach, Meshack, and Abednego. Rest assured of God's presence. He will see you through and establish His greatness in you. He is God, who can do all things for those who believe and trust Him.

Friends, let these words be engraved in your hearts: "Trust in the Word and promises of God." The promises of God for human salvation are the reason for the manifestation of our Lord and Saviour, Jesus Christ, on the earth, and the reason He climbed the tree of anguish at Calvary to die in our place. Our sins were nailed to the cross with Him to grant us victory, freedom from the captivity of the Devil, and eternal life. The Bible says, 'Surely he took up our infirmities and carried our sorrows, yet we considered him stricken by God. But he was pierced for our iniquities; the punishment that brought peace was upon him, and by his wounds we are healed' (Isa. 53:4–5).

The truth is that you have no faith until it is tested with fire and you still remain faithful to God.

> The truth is that you have no faith until it is tested with fire and you still remain faithful to God.

Father Lord, I pray that those who read this book will not miss the fulfilment of Your promises to them. I pray that they will not be defeated by the Devil during their trials and afflictions. In Jesus's name, amen.

CHAPTER 1

In the Beginning

The history of creation according to the book of Genesis did not contain the origin of God. No scriptural account or scientific record describes the beginning of God. The first verse of the Bible presents us with God already in existence. The rest of the Scripture is an expansion on the theme of who God is, what He is like, and what He is doing.

God has no beginning. He is eternal, without beginning and without ending. He brings about the beginning of all things through His Word. He is the Creator of heaven and the earth. – Elohim. He is the beginning of all beginnings, and the fountain of all things. His sovereignty is eternal.

The eternity of God is difficult for the human mind to comprehend, since humans are rooted in time and accustomed to measuring life by the passage of time.

Eternity is not simply unlimited time forever; eternity is another dimension of existence. It belongs solely to God. It existed when He had not yet created time, and will continue to exist when time and season cease. God stands above time and season just as He stands above matters and persons. Time itself is God's creation.

No human is qualified to speak with certainty of the origin of God. The Bible says, 'Where were you when I laid the foundation of the earth? Tell me, if you have understanding' (Job 38:4). Only God Himself can give authoritative information about Himself. The book of Genesis simply tells us that 'God said', 'God saw', 'God divided', 'God called', 'God made', 'God created', 'God set', and 'God blessed'. There isn't any reference to His origin. That is why He is called 'the incomprehensible and invisible God'.

God promised Moses that His presence would go with him (Exod. 33:14). But He also said to Moses, 'You cannot see my face, for no one may see me and live' (Exod. 33:20).

The Nature and Attributes of God

Talking about the attributes of God means talking about His nature in His manifested character. God's attributes are many, as set forth in the Scripture. The attributes of God are those peculiarities which define the mode of His existence or His character.

God the Creator – Elohim
The Bible says that in the beginning, God created the heaven and the earth (Gen. 1:1). He has no beginning, but He brought about the beginning of all things through His spoken word as Creator.

God Is Spirit
This is the exact word from our Lord Jesus Christ in John 4:24, showing that God is purely, wholly, and only Spirit, who does not inhabit a body. Jesus said again after His resurrection,

'A spirit hath not flesh and bones as ye see me have' (Luke 24:39). We also know that God is pure Spirit because of His invisibility (Col. 1:15; 1 Tim. 1:17; Heb. 11:27). Because of His omnipresence, He gives His Spirit to man (Gen. 2:7; Acts 2:4).

God Is Love
The number one attribute that people love to embrace is the fact that God is love. This word condenses for us His mercy, grace, and loving-kindness. God loves all His creation. God wants to share a personal relationship with the human beings He created in His image and likeness. God does not just love; He *is* love.

In 1 John 4, there is extensive discussion about God's love, while the gospel passage John 3:16 expresses the love of God that has no end in the world.

God Is Holy
Though all the attributes of God are important and depend on one another, the fact of the holiness of God seems to be what God wants man to emphasise and emulate most. 'Be thou holy for I am holy' (1 Pet. 1:16; see also Lev. 11:44). When God revealed Himself – as He did to Moses, Job, and Isaiah, as well as at the transfiguration – God's holiness was mentioned in each encounter. Isaiah called God 'The Holy One of Israel' more than thirty times in the Bible. Psalm 99 says, 'The Lord of our God is Holy' (v. 9).

Sovereign God
God rules His creation with His sovereignty and love. He is free to do what He knows is best for humanity. God is in complete control of all creation but he has also given human beings free will to obey or reject His leading.

God demonstrated His sovereign power and authority over all creation in the first and second chapters of the Bible. He says, 'Let there be,' and it becomes so. The whole of the Bible shows how God exhibits His sovereign authority over all creation, including kings, kingdoms, the sea, and angels.

Trinity God

While God is One, He manifests Himself in three distinct persons: God the Father, God the Son, and God the Holy Spirit. The Trinity is taught in the Old Testament: 'In the beginning God-'The Father' created heaven and the earth and the earth was void and darkness was upon the deep and the Spirit- 'Holy Spirit' was hovering over the deep and God said 'The Word/God the Son, let there be light and there was light' (Gen. 1:1–3). God also referred to the Trinity when He said, 'Let us create man in our own image and after our likeness' (Gen. 1:26).

The doctrine of the Trinity is taught in the New Testament as well. During the baptism of Jesus Christ in Matthew 3, all three persons of the Trinity appear: the Father speaks as the Holy Spirit descends upon Jesus Christ from heaven. Jesus also mentioned the Trinity in the Great Commission given to the church: 'Therefore, go and make disciples of all nations, baptizing them in the name of the Father, the Son and the Holy Spirit' (Matt. 28:19). Jesus later says that he will ask His Father to send the Holy Spirit as a Comforter and Counsellor (John 14:16). The Bible makes several statements that each one of the three persons are God (for the Father, see Rom. 1:7; for the Son, see Heb. 1:8; for the Spirit, see Acts 5:3–4).

Immutable God
By His nature, God is absolutely unchangeable. He remains the same before the creation of heaven and earth as He is today and forever will be till eternity, without end. Psalm 90:2 says that before the mountains were born or He brought forth the earth and the world, from everlasting to everlasting, He is God.

The God who created all things never changes; hence His Word is infallible.

Righteous God
God's holiness is manifested in His righteousness. God is holy because He is righteous; He expresses His holiness in the way He deals with humanity. Psalm 116.5 and Ezra 9:15 say that God is righteous. Many other Bible verses, such as Exodus 9:23–27, Psalm 129:4, Jeremiah 12:1, and 1 John 1:9, declare God's righteousness.

Merciful God
God's mercy has been defined as Jehovah Elohim, the Creator, who does not give humanity what they deserve. Human beings, as sinners, deserve eternal damnation and expulsion from the presence of God forever, but God in His mercy chose to offer sinners salvation and eternal life. God is merciful, and His mercy endures forever (Deut. 4:31; Ps. 1–3:8; Eph. 2:4; Rom. 5:8). The parable of the Prodigal Son in Luke 15 gives a beautiful picture of God's mercy to humanity.

Omnipotent God
God by His omnipotence has no limit. He is able to do all things that He chooses to do. God has no limitations except the ones He places on Himself. He possesses absolute power that

is greater than all the powers in heaven and the earth together. The Bible says, 'I know that you can do all things; no plan of yours can be thwarted' (Job 42:2). This is the declaration of God's sovereignty, recognising His unlimited power to do all things.

Genesis 18:14 simply asks if there is anything too hard for the Lord. The answer is no. God has demonstrated His omnipotent power since the beginning of creation and throughout all the past six dispensations

Omnipresent God
God's omnipresence confirms that He is in all places at all times, both in heaven and on earth. His throne is in heaven, but He is also present everywhere else to intervene in all affairs. Proverbs 15:3 says that His eyes are all over the place. Jeremiah 23:23–24 says that God is close at hand and that no one can hide himself from God. The psalmist says that he can never be out of the sight of God (Ps. 139:7–12).

Omniscient God
God has knowledge of everything, and His knowledge is complete. Nothing is hidden for our God. Whether in the depth of the sea or inside a rock or in the wilderness or under the earth, all things are visible to almighty God. This is why God is called omniscient.

Faithful God
The faithfulness of God is true and has been proven several times in the Bible. God is immutable and His word is infallible. The highest reason for God's covenants with Noah, Abraham, Isaac, Jacob, and David, later personified in Jesus Christ, the Son of

God, was the Word He pronounced (Gen. 1:26–28). Hebrews 6:18 says: 'God cannot lie, nor can He break an unconditional promise that he says he will fulfil.' Every covenant God makes is kept; all His promises are fulfilled and prophecies achieved.

Evidence and testimonies of God's faithfulness are found throughout the Bible. 'Know therefore that the Lord your God is God; he is the faithful God, keeping his covenants of love to a thousand of those who love him and keep his commandments' (Deut. 7:9). In fact, the accounts of God's covenant with His people can be found in over 270 passages.

Though the Jews were scattered around the world, God promised in the Old Testament that they would return to the land he gave to Abraham, Isaac, Jacob, and all their descendants (Zech. 8:7–8; Ezek. 37:1–14). The promise came to fulfilment in 1948 when the nation of Israel was born again. 'Before the mountains were brought forth or ever thou art form the earth and the world, even from generation to generation, thou art God' (Ps. 90:2).

Forgiving God
Forgiveness is the expression of God's love, grace, and mercy over his ensnared children, setting them free from bondage to fulfil destiny. The power of forgiveness is beyond human comprehension, just as the love and the grace of God are immeasurable and incomparable. The Bible says, 'But God demonstrates his own love for us, in that while we were yet sinners, Christ died for us' (Rom. 5:8).

In disobedience to God, man formed an alliance with Satan to scuttle the perfect creation. But with love, grace, and mercy, He gave His only begotten Son as living sacrifice.

I delve more extensively into this subject in my books *Christian Marriage and Family Life* and *Holy Spirit: The Abiding God*.

God's names are Elohim, Yahweh, Jehovah God, the Ancient of Days, the Everlasting God, The I Am that I Am, the Creator of Heaven and Earth, the Immortal and Invisible God, the almighty God, God and Father of All, God and Father of our Lord Jesus Christ, the Most High God, God of Glory, God of Heaven, God of Hope, God of All Flesh, the Merciful God, God of Love and Peace, the Everlasting God, Everlasting Father, Faithful Creator, Father of the Fatherless, the Consuming Fire, the Gracious Father, the Father of Israel, the Jealous God, the Greatest Warrior, the Shadow from the Heat, the Sure Foundation, Abba Father, the Shelter for the Homeless, the Provider, the Protector, the Author of Peace, Aged but not Old, He Is Light, and He Is Faithful and Trustworthy.

God spoke His Word to fabricate the fullness of the universe, including all the unseen spirits, the angelic beings, and the physical things that we can see through His creative power (Ps. 148:1–12). He ordained all things to function as He desired them to be. Creation is the purposeful act of God; it is not like an unwanted pregnancy. God ordered it, planned it, and created all things for His glory.

God Himself is the highest reason for living; He is the highest end of life. The Bible says, 'You are worthy, O Lord. To receive glory and honour and power, for you created all things, and by your will they exist and were created' (Rev. 4:11). God is the finality of life and the final consummation of all things. He is the fountain and the end of our lives.

Hebrew Names of God and their Meanings

Names	Meanings
Adonai Jehovah	The Lord our Sovereign
El-Elyon	The Lord Most High
El-Olam	The Everlasting God
El-Shaddai	The God who is sufficient for the needs of His people
Jehovah-Elohim	The eternal Creator
Jehovah-Jireh	The Lord our provider
Jehovah- Nissi	The Lord our banner
Jehovah-Ropheka	The Lord our healer
Jehovah-Shalom	The Lord our peace
Jehovah-Tsidkenu	The Lord our righteousness
Jehovah-Mekaddiskem	The Lord our sanctifier
Jehovah-Sabaoth	The Lord of Hosts
Jehovah Shammah	The Lord is present
Jehovah-Rohi	The Lord our Shepherd
Jehovah-Hoseenu	The Lord our Maker
Jehovah Eloheenu	The Lord our God

God the Son

The doctrine of Trinity in Christian theology identifies Jesus as God the Son and the second person of the Trinity. The Son of

God is one with God the Father and God the Holy Spirit from the beginning, but is distinct in person.

God the Son is coeternal with God the Father and God the Holy Spirit, before creation and after creation, until eternity and without end. The Bible says, 'In the beginning God "The Father" created the heavens and the earth. Now the earth was formless and empty, darkness was over the surface of the deep and the Spirit of God "Holy Spirit" was hovering over the waters. And God said "the WORD" let there be light and there was light' (Gen. 1:1–3).

The Word

The above passage confirms that when God spoke His Word, He got all He wanted. Nothing is said about the instrument or materials he used to create the world and all of its creatures. The Bible only says that God spoke His Word and it happened. Therefore, the Word of God is the only effective tool or instrument used by God to create the fullness of the earth and to bless humanity. The Word is the creative machinery of God.

The beauty of life is in knowing the truth (John 8:21). The truth is the Word of God (John 17:17) personified in the person of Jesus Christ (John 1:14). The Word is interconnected to all living organisms, both in heaven and on the earth. Without Him, nothing is created (John 1:4).

Regrettably, He came to that which was His own, but His own did not receive Him. Yet to all who received Him, to those who believed in His name, He gave the right to become the children of God (John 1:11–12).

The gospel of John explores what it means to believe and confess that Jesus is the Word, the creative power of God, the Christ, the Son, and the Lamb of God. John's gospel explains: 'In the beginning of "Creation" was the WORD, and the WORD was with God, and the WORD was God, He was with God in the beginning. Through Him "The WORD" all things were made; without Him "The WORD" nothing was made that has been made' (John 1:1–3).

John's account of Jesus Christ as the Word and God stretches back to the beginning, beyond time and into eternity, to establish the deity of our Lord Jesus Christ as the Word of God and God incarnate.

The Bible says, 'Through Him all things were created, without Him nothing was made that has been made' (John 1:3) This is a revelation about Jesus, who is the Son, the Lamb, and the Word of God. He is the fountain and architect of life. Suffice it to say that all creatures, including humans, are the product of the Word.

The Bible says further, 'In him 'The WORD' was the life, and that life was the light of men, the light shine in the darkness and the darkness cannot comprehend it' (John 1:4–5). Understanding the revelatory truth about the Son of God who is the Word of God personified in our Lord Jesus Christ is the key needed to unravel the misery of life and unlock all that God had in stock for humanity.

'In Him was the life': life itself is the gift of God freely given to man, so that man can be like God and represent His image on earth. Through the Word, God designed every cell in human DNA to obey Him so we can be blessed (Deut. 28:1).

The Word of God contains eternal life, with the power to destroy all that was not created, such as sin, sickness, death, and all the manifestations of darkness. The Word brings about miracles, signs, and wonders. 'And that life was the light of men and the light shines in the darkness but the darkness cannot comprehend it' (John1:4–5).

The Word is matter and the light is energy. When the Word is spoken, it goes out with the power of illumination, energy, revelation, dreams visions, ideas, insights, wisdom, knowledge, understanding, blessing, and prosperity. The Word of God is the truth of life, interconnected to all things. The Word is the fountain of a life-giving river. All things begin, revolve around, and end with the Word of God. Thus Jesus declared, 'I am the Alfa and the Omega, says the Lord God, "who is, and who was, and who is to come, the Almighty' (Rev. 1:8).

The power of the spoken Word of God is one of life's greatest mysteries. Hence the birth, death, resurrection, and ascension of the Son of God remain mysteries to the unbelievers. The likeness of God simply demands that the Word of God should be engrafted in our spirit-man so we can recreate the world around us to reflect God's image and likeness. The Bible says, 'The word became flesh and made his dwelling among man and we behold his glory, the glory of the only begotten Son, full of glory' (John 1:14).

The Son of God manifested so He could offer Himself as a living sacrifice on the cross at Calvary to redeem the world.

This is why Jesus Christ says, 'I am the light of the world' (John 8:12).

The Word of God is power and can pierce through any barrier. It can split the rock and quake the depths of the sea. The Word of God travels 186,000 miles per second with a higher degree of illumination than ordinary light. It is called the *shekinah* glory. The Bible records phrases such as the voice of the Lord is over the waters; the God of glory thunders; the Lord thunders over the mighty waters; the voice of the Lord is powerful; the voice of the Lord is majestic; the voice of the Lord breaks the cedars; the Lord breaks in pieces the cedars of Lebanon. (See Ps. 29:3–5.)

The spoken Word of God creates and alters existence to reshape the world He makes. God commanded Moses to stretch the rod in his hand over the sea and speak His Word to divide the Red Sea. The sea heard the Word, and a pathway was created for the children of God to walk on the dry land amid the sea (Exod. 14:21–31).

The Word of God was released over the dry bones in the valley, and resurrection happened (Ezek. 37:1–14). Jesus released the Word over dead-and-buried Lazarus, and he who died and was buried rose from the grave. Jesus released the Word over those afflicted with sickness, diseases and demon possession, and they all received healing and deliverance (Matt. 4:23–24).

Jesus also commissioned His disciples with the power of the Word and sent them out to heal all manner of sickness and cast out demons (Matt. 10:1).

When Jesus Christ declared the Word on the cross at Calvary and said, 'It is finished,' the entire creation quaked, rock split, graves opened to release the dead, and they truly rose. The curtain that prevented man from entering into the Holy of Holies got torn from top to bottom, giving humanity the grace to be in the presence of God again, as they had been in the garden of Eden (Matt. 27:50–53).

The Bible says, 'The voice "WORD" of the Lord strikes with flashes of lightening. The voice "word" of the Lord shakes the deserts; the Lord shakes the desert of Kadesh. The voice 'word' of the Lord twists the oaks and strips the forests bare. And in his temple all cry, "Glory"' (Ps. 29:7–9). This was the very reason our Lord Jesus Christ declared, 'I am the resurrection and the life, he who believes in me will live, even though he dies, and whoever lives and believes in me will never die. Do you believe this?' (John 11:25–26).

This is the truth of the gospel and the reason Jesus specifically gave the church the Great Commission: to go and make disciple of all nations, teaching them to obey the Word (Matt. 28:19–20; Mark 16:15–18; Acts 1:8). You will know the truth and the truth will set you free (John 8:32).

Jesus also declared that the Word of God is the truth and made a valuable illustration on the importance of the Word of God (John 17:17). He says, 'I am the true vine and my Father is the gardener' (John 15:1). He says further, 'Remain in me "The Word" and I will remain in you, no branch can bear fruit on itself, it must remain in the vine. Neither can you bear fruit unless you remain in the me I am the vine, you are the branches, if a man remain in me and I in him, he will bear much fruit, apart from me you can do nothing' (CITATION). Bearing fruit requires abiding in the Son of God and drawing on His sustaining grace.

There are over forty places in the New Testament where Jesus is given the title 'the Son of God' to draw our attention to His humanity. 'God the Son' refers more generally to His divinity, including His pre-incarnate existence. So, in Christian theology, Jesus was always God the Son.

The author of the epistle to the Hebrews, in his description of Jesus as the exact representation of the divine Father and the Son, says. 'Your throne, O God, will last for ever and ever' (Heb.1:8). This also has parallels in the epistle to the Colossians: 'In Christ all the fullness of the Deity lives in bodily form' (Col. 2:9).

John's gospel quotes Jesus at length regarding His relationship with His heavenly Father. It also contains two famous attributions of divinity to Jesus: 'The Word was God' (1:1), and the occasion when Thomas said to Him, 'My Lord and my God!' (20:28).

A few of His names are the King of Kings, the Lord of Lords, the Lion of Judah, the Root of David, the Messiah, the Redeemer, Christ our Lord, King of the Jews, Lord and Saviour, the Ancient of Days, the Chief Cornerstone, the Great High Priest, Emmanuel, Rock of Ages, the Merciful God, the Strength of the Poor, a Sure Foundation, Wonderful, Counsellor, the Advocate, Alpha and Omega, the Beginning and the End, Bread of Life, the Living Waters, the Light of the World, Friend of Sinners, Everlasting Father, Everlasting King, Everlasting God, Hope of Israel, Hope of Believers, the Wisdom of God, the Lamb of God, the Good Shepherd, the Mediator, the Only Begotten Son, the Prince of Peace, the Root of Jesse, Salvation of God, Saviour of the World, the Offspring of the Woman, the Bridegroom, the True Vine, and the Word.

The most direct references to Jesus as God are found in letters by Apostle Paul: 'Christ, who is God over all' (Rom. 9:5) and 'Our great God and Saviour, Jesus Christ' (Titus 2:13). We also have 'For to us a child is born, to us a Son is given and the government will be on His shoulders and He will be called Wonderful Counsellor, Mighty God, Everlasting Father, Prince of Peace' (Isa. 9:6). There is also, 'A voice came from the cloud, saying, "This is my Son whom I have chosen, listen to Him"' (Mark 9:35).

Jesus Christ is the Son of God and the true manifestation of God in human form (John 1:14). He came to destroy every work of darkness, to open the gates of prison, to set man free, and to restore the Spirit of God, bringing all that was misaligned into divine alignment with God.

God the Holy Spirit

The Holy Spirit is the third member of the Trinity Godhead. He is a person equal in every way with God the Father and God the Son. The Holy Spirit is the Spirit of God who came to reside within believers through Jesus Christ. He is the breath of God, breathed into the nostrils of humankind, that made man become a living soul at creation.

The Holy Spirit is what humanity lost at the hill of our disobedience in the garden of Eden, which led to human spiritual death. The same was released on the day of Pentecost, after Jesus rose from the dead and ascended to heaven (Acts 2:4). Jesus told His apostles, 'I will ask the Father, and He will give you another Helper, that He may be with you forever; the Spirit of truth, whom the world cannot receive, because it does not behold Him or know Him, but you know Him because He abides with you, and will be in you. I will not leave you as orphans; I will come to you' (John 14:16–18).

God is Father, Son, and Holy Spirit. All the divine attributes ascribed to the Father and the Son are equally ascribed to the Holy Spirit. When a person becomes born again by believing and receiving Jesus Christ as Lord and Saviour, such believers receive the baptism of the Holy Spirit, the abiding Spirit of God (1 Cor. 3:16; Matt. 3:11).

The Holy Spirit has intellect (1 Cor. 2:11). He has emotion (Rom. 15:30). He has will (1 Cor. 12:11). A primary role of the Holy Spirit is that He bears witness of Jesus Christ (John 15:26, 16:14). He speaks into people's hearts the truth about Jesus

Christ. The Holy Spirit also acts as a teacher (1 Cor. 2:9–14). He reveals God's will and God's truth to all believers.

Jesus told His disciples, 'The Helper, the Holy Spirit, whom the Father will send in My name, He will teach you all things, and bring to your remembrance all that I said to you' (John 14:26). Jesus revealed further, 'When He, the Spirit of truth, comes, He will guide you into all the truth; for He will not speak on His own initiative, but whatever He hears, He will speak; and He will disclose to you what is to come' (John 16:13).

The Holy Spirit was given to abide with believers in order to produce God's characters in a way that we cannot do on our own. The Holy Spirit will build into our lives love, truth, joy, peace, patience, kindness, goodness, faithfulness, gentleness, and self-control (Gal. 5:22–23). Rather than trying to be loving, patient, and kind on our own, God asks us to rely on Him to produce these qualities in our lives.

Thus Christians are told to walk in the Spirit (Gal. 5:25) and be filled with the Spirit (Eph. 5:18). The Holy Spirit empowers Christians to perform responsibilities that promote spiritual growth among Christians (Rom. 12; 1 Cor. 12; Eph. 4).

The Holy Spirit performs a function for non-Christians as well. He convicts people's hearts of God's truth concerning how sinful we are; of the need for God's forgiveness; of how righteous Jesus is and His death in our place on the cross at Calvary for our sins; and of God's eventual judgement of the world and those who do not know Him (John 16:8–11). The Holy Spirit troubles our hearts and minds to demand our repentance and turn us to God for forgiveness, to receive a new life.

Other names of the Holy Spirit are Comforter, Testifier, Teacher, Helper, Convector, Guardian, Declarer, Speaker, and Glorifier.

Jesus, the Son of God, declared after His resurrection that He had defeated Satan, claiming back the power that Adam lost in the garden of Eden and obtaining victory for all believers' humanity, He said, 'All authority has been given to Me in heaven and on earth. Go therefore and make disciples of all the nations, baptizing them in the name of the Father and the Son and the Holy Spirit, teaching them to observe all that I commanded you; and lo, I am with you always, even to the end of the age' (Matt. 28:18–20).

After His resurrection and before He ascended into heaven, Jesus spoke to His disciples and advised them to remain in Jerusalem until His Father sent the Holy Spirit to them to baptise them (Acts 1:5). He told them that they would be empowered to preach the gospel, from Jerusalem to the uppermost part of the world (Acts 1:8). The Spirit-filled church is thus empowered to share the gospel of Jesus Christ and enable the expansion of the church.

The baptism of the Holy Spirit to the church at Pentecost is also confirmed by the promises found in the Old Testament: 'And afterward, I will pour out my Spirit on all people. Your sons and daughters will prophesy, your old men will dream dreams, your young men will see visions' (Joel. 2:28).

This same Spirit is what Jesus promised to his disciples: 'John answered them all, "I baptize you with water. But one more powerful than I will come, the thongs of whose sandals I am not worthy to untie. He will baptize you with the Holy Spirit and with fire'" (Luke 3:16). 'But I tell you the truth, it is for your good that I am going away. Unless I go away, the Counsellor will not come to you; but if I go, I will send him to you' (John 16:7).

Man, the Image and the Likeness of God

The creation of humanity in the image and likeness of God brought God's creative activities to a climax and revealed the uniqueness and significance of created man. 'Then God said let's create man in our image and likeness' (Gen. 1:26).

God moved from commanding to consulting with His supreme council chamber – God the Father, God the Son, and God the Holy Spirit – for deliberation when He wanted to create man. In the previous works of creation, His divine Word expressed His divine will. He said, 'Let there be,' and His commandments were confirmed with words of accomplishment that followed: 'And it was so.' But when he approached the most excellent of creation, God consulted. This also suggests that though God is one absolute being, He is not solitary or single.

Before the creation of heaven and earth, God had the picture of the human beings to be created in His image and likeness at heart. He conceived humanity as those to whom He would give authority to manage the earth.

While drawing the sketch of the universe, like a woman would visualise the life of the baby in her womb, God was also visualising 'the man-god' to be created to rule over the kingdom of the earth.

Man is distinguished from the other creatures. 'God moulded the dust of the ground' to form man and breathed His Spirit into the nostrils of man, and man became a living being (Gen. 2:7). However, since man is the dust of the ground and only became a living being through the gift of God's Spirit, it is God's absolute right and privilege to know the time a woman conceives and the time of a person's birth or demise. Life is exclusively at the discretional will of God. He gives and takes when He wills.

The Bible says that 'all creation bear witness to the glory of God' (Ps. 19:1). But humanity above all things expresses and represents God on earth in righteousness, holiness, wisdom, knowledge, power, and understanding (Eph. 4:24; Col. 3:10). Humanity carries the blessing of fruitfulness and multiplication, to subdue and have dominion. The differences between human beings and the rest of the creatures on earth is emphasised in this phrase: 'according to His likeness and in His image'. In every respect, human beings are created to be like the heavenly Ruler. The Bible says, 'I praise you because I am fearfully and wonderfully made, your works are wonderful, I know that full well' (Ps. 139:14 NIV).

God also pictured a throne, which He eventually established in the garden of Eden for the 'god-man'. He planted a garden of His choice around the throne, with trees producing fruits of various types and waters running the length of Eden. Surely, the garden of Eden was a place of comfort, enjoyment, and relaxation. God used this well-watered place to produce special fruits and vegetation for the god-man on earth.

In such a place with abundance of water, every plant was pleasant to the sight and good for food (Gen. 2.9). Indeed, God's plan for man from inception was perfect–good and not evil. God provided waters and fish in the sea, birds in the air, beasts and crawling creatures on the land, vegetation for food, and the sun, moon, and stars for seasonal needs. All were perfectly put in place for the use of the god-man to be created.

God reproduced Himself in man and expected man to produce and speak things into existence with the Word of blessing, like God did. Not curse. 'The highest heavens belong to the Lord, but the earth He has given to man' (Ps. 8:3–4).

Let us draw attention to the dignity and uniqueness of the nature of human kind. The Lord God formed man from the dust of the ground and breathed the breath of life into his nostrils, and man became a living being (Gen. 2:7). God blessed them and said to them, be fruitful and increase in number, fill the earth and subdue it. Rule over the fish of the sea and the birds of the air and over all the living creatures that moves on the ground (Gen. 1:28).

That God did not consult with angels when He decided to create man in His image and likeness, after He had sufficiently made provision for human living, suggests that God never intended that humanity should be subject to angels. Human beings should never suffer or be poor, but should be blessed and prosper. The words of the prophet confirm God's perfect will and love for man: 'Who has directed the Spirit of the Lord or as his counsellor has taught him? With whom did he take counsel, and who instructed Him?' (Isa. 40:13–14).

King David wrote concerning this wonderful love for the god-man: 'When I consider your heavens, the work of your fingers, the moon and stars, which you have ordained. What is man that you are mindful of him, and the son of man that you visit him?' (Ps. 8:3–4)

Man was uniquely, fearfully, and wonderfully created with dominion over all the kingdoms of beasts, birds, fish, and plants, including all the crawling creatures, while the angels served as messengers for God to bless and protect man. Therefore, man was made to serve God alone and rule over all earthly creatures. It is an unthinkable abomination for a man to serve and to worship what he was created to dominate, or for man to worship angels. It is spiritual blindness to do so.

Consequences of Disobedience

God established a throne in the garden of Eden, upon which man was enthroned as king to rule over the fullness of the earth. Unfortunately, man lost this grace like the Prodigal Son. Man abused the unquantifiable privilege and grace of God; he rubbished the glory that was freely given at creation. Subsequently, man fell from the throne due to his disobedience to God's commandments.

Mercifully, the blessings and dominion man lost due to disobedience were restored by God through covenant-promise with humanity, culminating in the manifestation of the person of Jesus Christ, the Son of God.

Before the fall in the garden of Eden, Adam and Eve had perfect communion with God. But their amazing fellowship was broken due to human acts of disobedience to God's commandments, and they were separated from God (spiritually dead). They became conscious of their sin and were ashamed and hid themselves from God (Gen. 3:8–10). Man has been hiding from God ever since.

Only through Jesus Christ, the Son of God, and the Holy Spirit can that fellowship be restored. In Him, we have become righteous and sinless in God's eyes, as Adam and Eve were before they sinned. 'God made him who had no sin to be sin for us, so that in him we might become the righteousness of God' (2 Cor. 5:21).

Because of the fall, spiritual and physical death became realities. All creation was subject to death because the life-giving Spirit of God had disappeared from man.

When Adam and Eve chose to disobey their Creator, they lost their innocence. Their minds were darkened by sin. The Bible says, 'Since they do not think it worthwhile to retain the knowledge of God, He gave them over to a depraved mind' (Rom. 1:28).

The other effect of the fall was the loss of sight, the very purpose for which man was created, which is to always be in the presence of God, to glorify Him, and to enjoy His presence forever. The Bible says, 'For from him and through him and to him are all things. To him be the glory forever. Amen' (Rom. 11:36). 'All the nations you have made will come and worship before you, O Lord; they will bring glory to your name' (Ps. 86:9). Selfishness became the essence of man after the fall, but God's loving-kindness stands forever.

Satan, the Devil, then stole human blessings and took over the life and the world that had been freely given to man by God. Satan clouded human minds and continues to manipulate human hearts with doubt and fear. Satan causes man to be subjective and to worship creatures –beasts and birds – as well as the sun, moon, stars, and plants that man was originally created to rule over. The heart of man was darkened and full of evil and wickedness.

CHAPTER 2

The Genesis of Promises

What would be the reaction and feelings of any king or parents who had invested so much into the life of their loved son from childhood to adulthood, built him a mansion within their empire, spent lavishly for his wedding, and ultimately given him dominion to manage their empire, only to find the same son in the street, living under a tree as a mad person? I pray that this will not be the portion of anyone in Jesus's Name. But that is horrible, isn't it?

That was the experience of God concerning the man He created in His image and likeness, the inhabitant of the garden of Eden, who was given rulership over the entire earth. Man was now dethroned, expelled, and barred from re-entry into the garden of Eden. The Bible says, 'After he drove the man out he placed on the east side of the Garden of Eden a Cherubim and a flaming sword flashing back and forth to guard the way to the tree of life' (Gen. 3:24).

Believers in Christ, let's consider the reason why Satan decided to deceive man. The Bible says, 'And there was war in heaven. Michael and his angels fought against the dragon, and the dragon and his angels fought back. But he was not strong enough and they lost their place in heaven. The great dragon was hurled down; that ancient serpent called the devil or Satan, who leads the whole world astray. He was hurled to the earth and his angels with him' (Rev. 12:7–9)

Now Satan and his fallen angels, or demons, had lost their places in heaven, while dominion to rule over the earth had already been given to man. Thus, Satan had lost all relevance, both in heaven and on earth, and had become a wanderer in the garden of the Lord. The only option left for him to become relevant again was to fight against man by stealing the dominion power given to humanity. Regrettably, he succeeded when he got man to eat the forbidden fruit.

Satan deceived Eve into taking the forbidden fruit. In turn, Ee took the fruit to her husband Adam, and both ate. They sinned by disobeying God's command.

Surely, God was disappointed, but His love for man remains. The garden of Eden, meant for the comfort of man, now became a courtyard where God sat on the throne of judgement to pronounce a guilty verdict. The first couple now became the accused. 'Adam, where are you?' The sinful man and his wife had gone into hiding. Regret set in, their consciences troubled them, and things fell apart. Man could no longer stand in the presence of God. The Spirit of God instantly disappeared from man at the bite of the forbidden fruit. Man became a natural soul-ish man instead of a supernatural spirit man.

The pronouncement of judgement upon the disobedient man and the serpent became God's only option. Man inherited the ultimate death penalty, but the content of the judgement against Satan provided an escape route for man. 'So the Lord God said to the serpent, because you have done this, "cursed are you above all the livestock and all the wild animals!;…all the days of your life. And I will put enmity between you and the woman, and between your offspring and hers; he will crush your head, and you will strike his heel' (Gen. 3:15). This is the beginning of all promises of salvation and restoration.

God laid the foundation of His irrevocable promises that will never fail: restoration of life, blessing, prosperity, and hope of returning to the garden of Eden. This is the full revelation of our Lord Jesus Christ and His final victory over Satan on the cross at Calvary. The ministry of our Lord Jesus Christ was established in the above Scripture. It is the first good news and the first promise of salvation for the fallen man.

God's judgement against Satan several thousand years ago includes the promise of victory and salvation for mankind. Who can discern His errors? Judgement against Satan produced another virgin Eve. After several thousand years, the virgin Eve manifested as virgin Mary. The offspring of the woman manifested in the person of Jesus Christ, the Son of the living God, the Lion of Judah from the root of David.

Before the birth of the promised offspring of the woman, Jesus Christ, God intermittently sent His Holy Spirit to work with His chosen men, starting from Noah and including Abraham, Isaac, Jacob, Moses, David, and all the prophets in the Bible. Through them, God unveiled His plans of salvation in covenant promises over several dispensations, as explained below.

Seven Scriptural Road Maps to the Fulfilment of God's Promises

Understanding the seven scriptural dispensations of God's covenant promises and their progressive fulfilment from Genesis to Revelation will give us practical knowledge of God's love, and a road map towards fulfilment of the great promises with full understanding of God's plan of salvation for humanity. It will also highlight the progressive revelations and fulfilment of the promises from Adam and Eve to Noah's and Abraham's dispensations and further to the pregnancy of Emmanuel, the Son of God; the birth of the Messiah; and the final defeat of the Devil by the Messiah's sacrificial death on the cross.

The final victory over Satan on the cross brings total redemption from the bondage of sin and its wages of death to mankind. It also reveals God's love for man as He progressively implements His programme of salvation to bring man back to the lost garden of Eden, otherwise known as paradise or the new heaven and earth, which is the dispensation of God's kingdom.

This approach will reveal the unity of the Bible's Old and New Testaments, showing the Old Testament conceived the New Testament and the New Testament reveals the Old Testament. They agree with each other to establish the systematic fulfilment of the covenant promises of God.

Also, it will ultimately reveal the unity and the undying love of God the Father, the Son, and the Holy Spirit for mankind, as it was in the beginning of creation and will be until eternity, without end.

God's Seven Milestones

1.	**Innocence**	Genesis ch. 2 to 3	The fall of man
2.	**Conscience**	Genesis ch. 3 to 7	The flood
3.	**Government**	Genesis ch. 8 to 11	The Tower of Babel
4.	**Promise**	Genesis ch. 12 to Exodus ch. 19	Egypt enslavement
5.	**Law**	Exodus ch. 20 to Acts ch. 2	Birth and crucifixion
6.	**Grace**	Acts ch. 2 to Revelation ch. 18	Apostasy
7.	**Kingdom**	Revelation ch. 19 to 22	Rebellion

The Promises of Grace

1.	**Innocence**	The seed of the woman
2.	**Conscience**	Noah's ark
3.	**Government**	The rainbow
4.	**Promise**	Call of Abraham, birth and sacrifice of Isaac
5.	**Law**	The temple
6.	**Grace**	The cross
7.	**Kingdom**	The millennial temple

Dispensation of Innocence

The dispensation of innocence extends from the creation of Adam in Genesis 2:7 to the expulsion from Eden. Humanity was living a perfect life with the Holy Spirit of God during this dispensation. The commandment of God was the obedience of man, His heartbeat was the feeling of man. There was unbroken fellowship.

Human beings did not need to labour to live; they lacked nothing because all needs were divinely supplied. There was no planting of crops and harvesting season because there were plenty of fruits and vegetation to eat. No hunger, no thirst, no pain, no sickness, no disease, no death: the world was a perfect place. Until the sin of disobedience entered life and man lost grace, the only labour required of humanity was to care for the garden and be in the presence of God to have sweet fellowship with the Creator.

The dispensation of innocence ended in the first failure of man, and its far-reaching effects were disastrous. It closed with the promise of salvation and the first judgement.

Revelation	God spoke with Adam and Eve directly.
Rules	Multiply, care for the garden, eat fruits, be nice to the animals. Do not eat of the tree of knowledge.
Blessings	No sin, perfect environment, sweet fellowship with God, meaningful work, plentiful food, animals are all friendly.
Judgement	Spiritual and eventual physical death, work for food, pain in childbirth, sinful nature, chased out of the garden.
Promise	The Messiah, "the offspring of the woman".

Dispensation of Conscience

The sin of disobedience to God's commandment marred the image and likeness of God in man, leading to human expulsion from the garden of Eden. Human beings were left to their consciences, to live according to their hearts' desires.

Regrettably, the thoughts in human hearts were always wicked, evil to the point that God regretted He created man (Gen. 6:5). Peace was conspicuously absent from the earth. Wickedness thrived among men. The dispensation of conscience marked the beginning of planting and harvesting by man and also marked the beginning of blood sacrifices of animals. It ended with the flood.

Revelation	Hope for the seed of the woman; sacrifices of animals.
Rules	Blood sacrifice for sin, looking forward to the seed of the woman, obedience, conscience, and no revenge for murder (Cain).
Blessings	Hope for a Saviour to be born, agricultural society, no government.
Judgement	The flood and total destruction, except for Noah's family.

Dispensation of Human Government

Out of the fearful judgement of the flood, God saved eight people to whom He gave the purified earth, with ample power to govern it. This dispensation of human government began with Noah's family and God's covenant promises to them of blessing and dominion to rule over all creatures, sealed with the covenant promise of the rainbow, by which God promised never again to destroy the earth with a flood (Genesis 9:16-17). Unfortunately, wickedness persisted. Murder and all manner of wickedness increased. Judgement was enforced; anyone who killed was to be killed. The animals became carnivorous and ate human beings.

Human government resolved to build the tower of Babel to reach up to God, contrary to God's directive for man to fill the surface of the earth. This dispensation of human government ended with the judgement of confusion of human tongues to mark the beginning of ethnicity, tribes, and division.

Revelation	Mankind given authority to rule themselves.
Rules	Murderers punished by death. Mankind can eat animals; some animals will eat man; mankind to multiply and spread over the earth.
Blessings	Rainbow, protection of government.
Judgement	Confusion of tongues at the tower of Babel.

Dispensation of Promise

Out of the dispersed descendants of the builders of Babel, God called one man, Abram, with whom He entered into covenant promise of blessings. Some of the promises given to Abram and his descendants were purely gracious and unconditional. Abram received the promise that he would become the father of a nation, and his descendants would become the fountain of blessing for all human generations, ultimately producing the Saviour of the world.

Some promises were conditional upon the faithfulness and obedience of the descendants of Abram. Unfortunately, some of the conditions were violated through unfaithfulness and disobedience. The dispensation of promise resulted in the failure of Israel and closed in the judgement of bondage in Egypt.

Revelation	The seed of Abraham will bless the world; Abraham will be father of many nations and the line of Christ.
Rules	Believe that God will send a Saviour and that the Hebrews are His people.
Blessings	Earthly abundance.
Judgement	Enslavement of Jews in Egypt, plagues of Egypt, freedom and conquest of Canaan.

Dispensation of Law

In the dispensation of law, the grace of God came to the help of the helpless descendants of Abraham. God redeemed the chosen children of Israel through Moses from out of the land of the oppressors in Egypt.

The Israelites were supposed to ride on the grace of God from Egypt to the Promised Land in forty days. But they were unfaithful, disobedient, and rebellious, and the journey was prolonged. In the wilderness of Sinai, God proposed the covenant of grace, but they asked for the law instead of accepting a continued relationship of grace. The law was given.

The history of Israel in the wilderness and in the Promised Land is one long record of flagrant and persistent violation of the law. For the Israelites, God closed the testing of man by law in judgement after several warnings. First the nation of Israel and then the nation of Judah were driven out of the land into dispersion. After a period of time, a remnant few returned to the land under Ezra and Nehemiah, during which time Jesus Christ, the promised offspring of the woman, was born of a virgin – made under the law.

The Jews and Gentiles conspired to crucify Him on the cross at Calvary.

Revelation	God spoke to Moses and the prophets in the Old Testament.
Rules	The law; strict judgement.
Blessings	Word of God, God's chosen people, theocracy.
Judgement	Destruction of the temple, Israel set aside by God.
Divine Sacrifice	The birth and crucifixion of our Lord to usher in grace.

Dispensation of Grace and the Church Age

The present dispensation of grace is also referred to as the dispensation of the church: 'For until the law sin was in the world, but sin was not imputed when there is no law. Nevertheless, death reigned from Adam to the dispensation of Law' (Rom. 5:13).

The sacrificial death of Jesus Christ our Lord on the cross at Calvary introduced the dispensation of grace. 'Grace' means unmerited favour or God-given righteousness, instead of God requiring righteousness as under the law. Salvation, perfection, and eternal life are now freely offered to Jews and Gentiles upon the acknowledgement of sin and repentance, with faith in Christ.

Jesus answered and said unto them, This is the work of God, that ye believe on him whom he hath sent. (John 6:29)

Verily, verily, I say unto you, He that believeth on me hath everlasting life. (John 6:47)

Verily, verily, I say unto you, He that heareth my word, and believeth on him that sent me, hath everlasting life, and shall not come into condemnation; but is passed from death unto life. (John 5:24)

My sheep hear my voice, and I know them, and they follow me: and I give unto them eternal life; and they shall never perish. (John 10:27–28)

For by grace are ye saved through faith; and that not of yourselves: it is the gift of God: Not of works, lest any man should boast. (Eph. 2:8–9)

The first event in the closing of this dispensation will be the descent of the Lord from heaven, when sleeping saints will be raised together with the living believers to meet the Lord in the sky. So shall we ever be with the Lord (1 Thess. 4:16–17). It will be followed by the brief period called 'the great tribulation'. (See Jer. 30:5–7; Dan. 12:1; Zeph. 1:15–18; Matt. 24:21–22.)

After this, the personal return of the Lord to the earth in power and great glory will occur. Judgements will introduce the seventh and last dispensation; the dispensation of God's kingdom will begin. (See Matt. 25:31–46; 24:29–30.)

Revelation	Jesus among us, apostle, and New Testament.
Rules	Grace, love, faith; Holy Spirit as guide for believers.
Blessings	Indwelling Holy Spirit and personal relationship with Christ.
Judgement	Destruction of false world and church

The Bible is divided into two segments, the Old and the New Testaments. Most but not all of the Old Testament pertains to the dispensation of law, while most but not all of the New Testament pertains to the dispensation of grace. The differences between the two dispensations are obvious.

Jesus said about the New Testament, 'This is my body which is given for you: this do in remembrance of me. Likewise also the cup after supper, saying, This cup is the new testament in my blood, which is shed for you' (Luke 22:19–20).

The New Covenant

The words *testament* and *covenant* have similar meaning. So the term *New Testament* can be translated *New Covenant*. Jesus said, 'This cup is the New Covenant in my blood.'

The Bible says, 'Behold, the days are coming, says the Lord, when I will make a new covenant with the house of Israel' (Jer. 31:31–37). 'I will put My law in their minds, and write it on their hearts ... they all shall know Me ... I will forgive their iniquity, and their sin I will remember no more' (Heb. 8:8–13, Heb. 10:3, 16–18).

The book of Hebrews was written to teach Jewish believers and the Gentile church that they no longer needed to keep the dispensation of law's lifestyle rules. There was likewise no need for the annual reminder of sin on the Day of Atonement, since a perfect sacrifice had been offered once for all by a perfect priest, Jesus Christ, who was without sin and superior to Aaron.

God also revealed the New Testament to Apostle Peter thus: 'Peter went up to the housetop to pray, he became hungry and fell into a trance and saw heaven opened and an object like a great sheet descending ... in it were all kinds of animal and a voice came to him, "Rise Peter, kill and eat!" But Peter said "Not so, Lord! For I have never eaten anything common or unclean." What God has cleansed, you must not call common' (Acts 10:9–48).

The Holy Spirit was then poured out on the Gentiles, and they spoke in tongues as a sign of indwelling Spirit. The tongues given were human languages, which were named in Acts 2:9–11. They signify the new blessing of the dispensation of grace, or church age, established on the day of Pentecost. The sign also revealed that the Gentiles were fully acceptable to God in the church, the body of Christ.

The first half of the book of Ephesians explains the new dispensation: 'Therefore remember that you, once Gentiles in the flesh ... were without Christ Jesus, you who once were far off have been brought near by the blood of Christ. For He Himself is our peace, who has made both one, and has broken down the middle wall of separation' (Eph. 2:11–14).

Galatians explains the new dispensation thus: 'I do not set aside the Grace of God; for if righteousness comes through the law, then Christ died in vain' (Gal. 2:21). 'Therefore, the law was our tutor, to bring us to Christ … but after faith has come, we are no longer under a tutor' (Gal. 3:24–25).

The book of Romans too talks about the new dispensation: 'But now the righteousness of God apart from the law is revealed, being witnessed by the law and the Prophets' (Rom. 3:21).

Dispensation of the Kingdom

After the purifying judgements that will attend the personal return of Christ to the earth, He will reign over the restored Israel and over the earth for one thousand years. This is the period commonly called 'the millennium'. The seat of His power will be Jerusalem. The saints, including the saved of the dispensation of grace – namely the church – will be associated with Him in His glory. (See Isa. 2:1–4; Isa. 11; Acts 15:14–17; Rev. 19:11–21; Rev. 20:1–6.)

But when Satan is 'loosed for a little season', he will find the natural heart as prone to evil as ever. He will easily gather the nations to battle against the Lord and His saints. This last dispensation will close, like all the others, in judgement. The great white throne will be set, the wicked dead will be raised and finally judged, and then the new heaven and a new earth will emerge. Eternity will then begin (Rev. 20:3, 7–15; Rev. 21; Rev. 22).

Revelation	Jesus on earth the second time as King of Kings.
Rules	Theocracy, with Messiah as King; restoration of the temple.
Blessings	World peace, righteous law, healing of nations.
Judgement	Destruction of rebellion, final judgement of all mankind

In every new dispensation:
- There is new revelation to man from God.
- There is a new set of lifestyle rules.
- There are new blessings and promises.
- There is a judgement for the failures of mankind at the end.

The seven-mile stone of the Scripture identifies every dispensation by the conditions above. Sometimes the Bible names the dispensation. 'All Scripture is given by inspiration of God, and is profitable for doctrine, for reproof, for correction, for instruction in righteousness' (2 Tim. 3:16).

The principles of previous dispensations are carried over, unless the revelation pertaining to a subsequent dispensation declares them to be nullified. So the Old Testament is valid. However, each dispensation builds on the one before, like a staircase climbing toward a higher understanding of God, ultimately to fulfil His great promises to humanity.

All of God's plan and promises glorify God for the benefit of humanity. God's sovereignty includes His ability to accomplish

His purpose, fulfil His promises, and deliver His people from all afflictions across several thousands of years in history.

God foretold the captivity of Abraham's descendants for four hundred years and promised their deliverance: 'Then the Lord said to him, "know for certain that your descendants will be strangers in a country not their own, and they will be enslaved and mistreated four hundred years. But I will punish the nation they serve as slaves, and afterward they will come out with great possession"' (Gen. 15:13–14).

The Israelites were the descendants of Abraham, a peculiar people often used by God to demonstrate His deliverance power. The deliverance of the Israelites from Egyptian slavery, led by Moses, was typology of human deliverance from the power of sin and captivity of the Devil, enabled by our Lord and Saviour, Jesus Christ.

God's Promises to Abraham

God began the process of fulfilling His great promise of salvation with a covenant promise with Abraham, the man acknowledged as a righteous and faithful man by God. 'The Lord had said to Abram, "leave your country, your people and your father's household and go to the land I will show you"' (Gen. 12:1).

Abram did not chose God or request that God choose him. God chose and invited Abram to a mission of blessing and to form a partnership with him, revealing and implementing His gracious redemptive plan for humanity through a covenant promise.

This was echoed by our Lord Jesus Christ as he spoke about the chosen one: 'You did not chose me but I chose you and appointed you to go and bear fruit, fruit that will last. Then the Father will give you whatever you ask in my name' (John 15:16).

The promise to Abram was in seven tiers:
1. I will make you unto a great nation
2. And I will bless you;
3. I will make your name great,
4. And you will be a blessing
5. I will bless those who bless you
6. And whoever curses you I will curse
7. And all peoples on earth will be blessed through you.

This covenant blessing of Abraham is twofold, carrying physical and spiritual breakthroughs, and ultimately focuses on the restoration of mankind, according to God's pronouncement in Genesis 3:15.

God's covenant promises were made with Abram in the context of commands to go out in faith, without thoughts of mutual agreement. It was one solemn command followed by seven promises. However, the blessings surely outweighed the demand for Abraham to leave all and follow the Lord.

This is what God has in store for those who obediently and faithfully love and follow His directive. The Bible declares, 'If you fully obey the Lord your God and carefully follow all his commands I give you today, the Lord your God will set you high above all the nations on earth. All these blessings will come upon you and accompany you if you obey the Lord your God' (Deut. 28:1–2).

Abraham faithfully believed and followed God's commands to obtain spiritual and eternal blessings that are always hidden in physical blessings. To know God and to be in a personal relationship with Him is the highest blessing of all.

I will make you unto a great nation
What a promise God made to a seventy-five-year-old man who had no child, yet received the assurance that he would become a nation. The dictionary defines a 'nation' as a community of people with common descent, history, and language, who form a state or a geographical territory. Abraham had no hope, but he had faith and trusted in God. God confirmed His promise for Abraham, who became the father of the nation of Israel, the chosen people. God is omnipotent indeed.

And I will bless you
The blessing of God has no limitation. It is all-encompassing. It includes wealth, health, favour, success, and prosperity. The Bible says: 'The blessing of the Lord makes one rich and he adds no sorrow to it' (Prov. 10:22).

Abraham secured the promise of blessing as he faithfully obeyed God's command. The Bible confirms it thus: 'Abraham had become very wealthy in livestock and in silver and gold' (Gen. 13:2).

We are serving a living and faithful God who cannot afford to lie or renege on His Word, which He exalts above His name. God is faithful from one generation to another generation.

I will make your name great
A great name in this context means a famous name. God fulfilled this promise in the lifetime of Abraham. Abraham's name became great. Over four billion Christians, Muslims, and Jews all over the world use the name of Abraham in prayers. The other person given a great name in the Old Testament is King David.

And you will be a blessing
This is a strong promise. It means Abraham's name will be used as a reference point in prayers: 'May God make me like Abraham' or 'God, let the blessing of Abraham be mine'. People and nations use Abraham's name in like manner: 'May God make us like Abraham.'

'Heaven and earth will pass away, but my words will not pass away' (Mark 13:31).

I will bless those who bless you
This denotes that those who dealt well with Abraham would receive God's favour, but whosoever dealt with Abraham cruelly would receive the wrath of God.

Beloved, all anointed men and women of God equally share this blessing. Whoever blesses the men and women of God will surely be blessed in return. No one who gives to anointed men of God will go unrewarded for their gift.

And whoever curses you I will curse
Whoever acted in a hostile way or dealt treacherously with Abraham, God cursed and punished. This promise was an assurance of protection against the aggression of the Wicked One.

This guarantee of protection was far more personal than the other promises. God was identifying Himself with Abraham and indicating that He would fight every battle of Abraham's life. Abraham had no battle of his own to fight; God was the warrior who fought every one. This is by extension the portion of anyone called by God into His marvellous grace.

Let's draw a few lessons from the various challenges faced by Abraham. The Bible says, 'And there was famine in the land and Abram went down to Egypt to live there for a while because the famine was severe' (Gen. 12:10).

One of the themes running through the history of Abraham, the early father of Israel, is the threat to the promises that God made. These promises are established with Abraham as bone of his bone and the flesh of his flesh – Sarah. But each time they ran into danger, God remained faithful and acted to safeguard His promises. He intervened to rescue Abraham and Sarah from the messes they found themselves in. For example: 'When the Egyptians see you, they will say, this is his wife, then they will kill me but will let you live. Say you are my sister, so that I will be treated well for your sake and my life will be spared because of you' (Gen. 12:12–13).

Though Pharaoh acted in ignorance when he took Sarah, he was still guilty of taking another man's wife. So 'the Lord plagued Pharaoh and his house with great plagues' (Gen. 12:17). The plague had the effect of protecting Abraham and Sarah. It seems that Pharaoh did not violate Sarah. He likewise took no revenge on Abraham, but allowed him to leave with all his possessions. 'And when Pharaohs officials saw her, they praised her to Pharaoh, and she was taken into his palace. He treated

Abraham well for her sake and acquired sheep and cattle, male and female donkeys, menservants and maidservants and camels. But the Lord afflicted serious diseases on Pharaoh and his household because of Abraham's wife Sarah' (Gen. 12:15–17).

The protection that God had promised was shown in Abraham's situation and made his original fears appear unfounded.

Testing time comes, and we are tempted to look away from God. Fears often grip us so that, instead of trusting God, we only see problems. We forget the faithfulness of God and end up bringing more trouble upon ourselves. Thank God that even when we are unfaithful, God remains faithful.

We see a similar pattern with Abimeleck, the king of Gerah (Gen. 20:1–18) and Isaac and the Philistines: 'And in you, all the families of the earth shall be blessed' (Gen. 26:6–11). This promise brings Abraham's blessing to all living human beings and all the nations of the world. One person, Abraham, is chosen and blessed in order that all nations of the earth might be blessed.

This promise finds its ultimate fulfilment in Jesus Christ: 'And you are heirs of the prophets and of the covenant God made with your fathers. He said to Abraham, through your offspring, all peoples on earth will be blessed' (Acts 3:25–26). As the sin of Adam affected the generations of humanity, so the blessing of Abraham carried ultimate blessing for the entire human race.

To your Descendants I Will Give This Land

The promise of land is already implied in the promises God gave to Abraham in Genesis 12:1, but here again, God is making it quite definite. Abraham will have descendants who will be given the land of Canaan as an inheritance from God.

God's promises are not based on what is seen in the physical world or what is within the range of possibility. His promises fall within the realm of what humans consider impossible.

God told Abraham to go out from his own country, to depart from his brethren and nation to become a father of a new generation of people – this at the age of 75, when he had no child of his own. Surely, my God is God of possibility. God declared to Abraham and to all believers that He is the God of possibility, the God who brought the whole universe into existence out of nothing. Is there anything too difficult for Him?

Jesus reaffirms this belief: 'I am the resurrection and the life, he who believes in me will live even though he dies; and whoever lives and believes in me will not die' (John 11:25).

Do you believe this wonderful promise of resurrection? Beloved, I don't know the challenges in your life. Seek the promise of God and stand on them. He'll do it at His appointed time.

> **Do not plan according to your knowledge and power; plan according to your God.** 'Now unto him who is able to do immeasurably more than all we ask or imagine, according to His power that is at work within us' (Eph. 3:20).

God, who brought the fullness of this earth into existence out of nothing, is able to do all things for those who trust and believe in Him. 'Great is our God and greatly to be praised, in the city of our God in the Holy mountain' (Ps. 40:1). None of His promises have ever failed. You only need trust and wait; He'll surely fulfil all He has promised.

The covenant of God for Abraham was confirmed to Isaac, Jacob, and David.

Barriers to Fulfilment of Promises

Our God is awesomely powerful and graciously wonderful, but He is a jealous God who will not share His glory with anyone. He created man and gave him dominion over all creatures, as well as the sun, moon and stars to serve him in seasons, and the soil to bear fruits and vegetation for our food.

If anyone turns around to use God's creation as a means of spiritual empowerment, then he or she has desecrated the temple of God, rubbished the glory of God, terminated the promises of God, and provoked God's furious jealousy.

The Bible says:

You shall have no other gods beside me. You shall not make for yourself an idol in the form of anything in heaven above or on the earth beneath or in the waters below. You shall not bow down to them or worship them; for I am the Lord your God punishing the children for the sin of the fathers to the third and fourth generation of those who hate me, but showing love to a thousand generations of those who love me and keep my commandments. (Exod. 20:3–6)

Let us be honest with ourselves. It does not matter who we are or what authority we possess in this world. God is the Creator and the fountain of life. He created man from the dust of the ground and breathed His Spirit into man's nostrils, and man became a living soul (Gen. 2:7). His sovereign authority sustains heaven and earth.

Only His Spirit enables us to have enduring blessings and prosperity. Other means are temporal. Gold and silver belong to God (Hag. 2:8).

The Bible says:

A third angel followed them and said in a loud voice. If anyone worship the beast and his image and receive his mark on the forehead or on the hand, he too will drink of the wine of God's fury, which has been poured full strength in the cup of the wrath. He will be tormented with burning sulphur in the presence of the holy angels and of the Lamb, and the smoke of their torment rises for ever and ever. There is no rest day or night for those who worship the beast and his image or for anyone who receive the mark of his name. (Rev. 14:9–11)

Human beings were not human until God created them. He will forever remain God, the Alpha and the Omega of our lives and everything else on earth. He has spoken very clearly: 'God blessed them and said to them, "Be fruitful and increase in number, fill the earth and subdue it. Rule over the fish of the sea and the birds of the air and over every living creature that moves on the ground"' (Gen. 1:28).

Friends, when you use any of the creatures – birds, fish, or beasts of the forest, including the crawling creatures such as snakes – as a source of power or object of worship, you have nullified or revoked the promises of God for your life. Jesus says, 'Yet a time is coming and has now come when the true worshippers will worship the Father in spirit and truth, for they are the kind of worshippers the Father seeks. God is Spirit and his worshippers must worship in spirit and truth' (John 4:23–24).

God is not to be worshipped through leaves, plants, birds, fish, mammals, or snakes. It is an abomination before God, and it is spiritual blindness. 'You shall have no other God beside me. You shall not make for yourself an idol in the form of anything in heaven above or in the earth beneath or in the waters below' (Exod. 20:3–4).

Worship your God in spirit and truth to accelerate the fulfilment of His promises in your life. Avoid making God jealous.

It takes a new mind to mind the things of God. 'Let this mind be in you, which was also in Christ Jesus' (Phil. 2:5).

God's Visitation

God moves in mysterious ways to bring His promises to fruition. God visited Abraham three times to affirm His covenant promises before their fulfilment. Beloved, each of God's promises carries the potency for miracles, signs, and wonders. His promises reveal what eyes have not seen, what ears have not heard, and what the mind has not thought of.

Every promise of God has the potency to bring life from death, light from darkness, wealth from poverty, hope from hopelessness, joy to the broken-hearted, and deliverance to the captive. Abraham lost every hope about the possibility of Sarah giving birth to a child because of her advanced age. He settled for Ishmael, the son of Hagai their maidservant. But God visited them at the moment of their hopelessness.

If God has established His covenant with you, there is nothing He will not do to ensure that His promises are fulfilled. His promises are settled, final, and irrevocable. Once fulfilment is established, God no longer speaks in the future tense of 'I will give', but in the present tense of 'I have given'.

God's promises give believers hope and visions for a better future. What believers must avoid or conquer within them as they walk with God are doubt, fear, and unbelief. These are the greatest enemies of the fulfilment of God's promises.

Let's consider this amazing experience of Abram in Genesis 15, when God visited him for the first time to re-establish His promise. 'Now when the sun was going down, a deep sleep fell upon Abram and behold terror and great darkness fell upon him' (Gen. 15:12).

This was a profound spiritual experience. Abram, an obedient, mature, and committed believer, went through 'terror and great darkness', similar to what many great men and women of God went through in the Bible. It's an experience that many believers must also go through. It is not a sign of immaturity or lack of commitment, but a period of trial, breakdown, and transformation.

A new dimension was added to Abram's experience: 'And it came about when the sun had set, that it was very dark, and behold, there appeared a smoking oven and a flaming torch which passed between these pieces' (Gen. 15:17).

People of God, if you find yourself in the darkness or the furnace, remember that this is where God refines and tests you. How you react will determine your destiny. 'Without faith no one can please God.' God said to Israel, 'Behold, I have refined you, but not as silver; I have tested you in the furnace of affliction' (Isa. 48:10). Precious metals can never be purified without intense heat.

In the midst of the overwhelming darkness to which Abram was subjected, a darkness that was both natural and supernatural, there came 'a flaming torch which passed between this pieces'. The flaming torch signified the manifestation of the Spirit of God corresponding to the 'seven lamps of fire ... which are the seven Spirits of God' before the throne of God (Rev. 4:5). It was at this moment of deepest darkness that God, in the appearance of a 'flaming torch', made His commitment to Abram.

Bear in mind, great people of Jehovah, that you may not arrive at your Promised Land until you pass through deep darkness and see the flaming torch of Jesus Christ. Whether your period of refining be short or prolonged (Abraham's was twenty-five years), you must wait for His promises. He will surely come, and His visitations may be repeated.

God visited Abram a second time to reaffirm His covenant of circumcision, to change the name of Abram to Abraham, meaning 'father of the multitude or many nations', and to change the name of Sarai to Sarah, meaning 'princess'.

God said to Abraham, 'As for Sarai your wife, you are no longer to call her Sarai. Her name will be Sarah. I will bless her and will surely give you a son by her. I will bless her so that she will become a mother of nations. Kings of people will come from her.'

Abraham fell face down. He laughed and said to himself, 'Will a son be born to a man a hundred years old? Will Sarah bear a son at the age of 90?'

Abraham said to God, 'If only Ishmael might live under your blessing.'

God said to Abraham, 'Yes, but your wife Sarah will bear you a son, and you will call him Isaac. I will establish my covenant with him as an everlasting covenant for his descendants after him.' (Paraphrased from Gen. 17:17–19.)

The Bible says, 'The nations will see your righteousness, and all kings your glory; you will be called by a new name that the mouth of the Lord will bestow' (Isa. 62:2).

God's visitations come at a time when the world has given up on you, at a point of rejection by friends and relatives, when solutions seem impossible.

Believers, the blessings of Abraham belong to you. God is coming to change your name from poor to wealthy, rich, blessed and prosperous; from barren to fruitful; from rejected to desired of men and women. Amen.

Of the third visitation Abraham received, the Bible tells us that the Lord appeared to him with a solution to Abraham's long-suffering hopelessness, again promising a child. This time around, it was Sarah who laughed in disbelief because of her age.

Perhaps you are in the position of Sarah? Wait and believe in the promise of God.

'The Lord appeared to Abraham near the great tree of Mamre while he was sitting at the entrance to his tent at the heat of the day' (Gen. 18:1). Abraham was probably dozing when he suddenly discovered that 'three men were standing by him'. Immediately, he rushed to greet them and 'bowed down to the ground for them'.

He offered the visitors the usual courtesy of Eastern hospitality: water to drink, water to wash their feet, a place to rest under a shady tree, and some light refreshment for their comfort as he urged them to wait for the main hospitality. Despite the midday sun, Abraham prepared a meal fit for kings: 'He then brought some curds and milk and the calf that had been prepared, and set these before them' (Gen. 18:8).

The Bible says, 'Do not forget to entertain strangers, for by so doing; some have unwittingly entertained angels' (Heb. 13:2). In Abraham's case, he actually entertained the Lord Himself and His angels without knowing whom he hosted. 'I was hungry and you gave me food ... in as much as you've did this to one of the least of these my brethren, you did it to me' (Matt. 25:35–40).

Abraham was warm-hearted, and he entertained his guests with the choicest food he could possibly offer. Only the finest wheat flour would do for the cake, and a top-quality calf was prepared for the table (Gen. 18:6–7). We are also called to give of our very best to the service of the Lord, which includes giving of our best to one another and generous giving to the life of the church.

After the meal, the Lord asked for Abraham's wife and made an announcement. "'Where is your wife Sarah?' they asked him. 'There in the tent' he said. 'I will surely return to you about this time next year and Sarah your wife will have a son!'" (Gen. 8:9–10).

Earlier in the book of Genesis, the emphasis was on Sarah's barrenness. Now we are told that Sarah had passed the age of child-bearing. According to human knowledge, it was no longer possible for Sarah to have a baby. 'So Sarah laughed to herself as she thought, "After I am worn-out and my master is old, will I now have this pleasure?" Then the Lord said to Abraham, "why, Sarah laughed and said, 'will I really have a child now that I am old?' Is anything too hard for the Lord, I will return to you at the appointed time next year and Sarah will have this pleasure'" (Gen. 18:12–14).

You Shall Be Called by a New Name

Names play significant roles in our lives. The name you bear carries some prophecy and often determines your destiny. The more people pronounce the prophecy in your name, the more it comes into manifestation.

In the lives of our patriarchs, God demonstrated how he changed names to bring about the fulfilment of His promises. Significantly, some names are associated with prophetic blessing, while other names are associated with curses because of their traditional, cultural, and religious background. For instance, a person whose name is associated with a god of thunder might be affected negatively because of the idolatrous association. The Bible says, 'You shall be called by a new name which the mouth of God shall mention' (Isa. 62:2b).

The name Abram means 'father' and was changed by God to Abraham, which means 'patriarch or father of a nation'. God changed Abram's name to prepare him for the fulfilment of the covenant. The Bible says, 'As for me, this is my covenant with you. You will be the father of many nations. No longer will you be called ABRAM. Your name shall be ABRAHAM for I have made you a father of many nations' (Gen. 17:4–5).

The use of the word 'fruitful' or 'multiply' in Genesis 1 is recalled in Genesis 17 for Abraham, just as it was confirmed to Noah in Genesis 9. Abraham, like Adam and Noah, stood at the beginning of an epoch in human history. God promised to make Abraham exceptionally fertile. Three times God promised that nations would emerge from Abraham. So his name was changed from 'father', exalted to 'father of many nations'.

We are told that Abraham's seed will include a royal line: 'and kings shall come from you'. Bible records show that Abraham eventually became the father of the Edomites, the Ishmaelites, and the Midianites, as well as the Israelites.

Promises were also made concerning Sarai, and her name was likewise changed.

Beloved readers, husbands and wives, are you learning from the history of Abraham and Sarah concerning God's promises?

Are you barren and have lost every hope of becoming a father or mother? Cheer up. He who promised is able to do it. He is God called Jehovah-Elohim, the Creator of all things. He can give you testimonies like that of Abraham and Sarah. Your waiting simply demands trust, obedience, and faith. Man may be unfaithful and lose hope, but God remains faithful. He will always make sure that His promises do not fail. 'I will establish my covenant as an everlasting covenant between me and you and your descendants after you for the generation to come to be your God and the God of your descendants after you' (Gen. 17:7–8).

Are you seeking the face of God in truth and in spirit, or are you seeking help from worldly powers in your distress? Know for sure that no man on earth could have healed Sarah of her barrenness, renewed her organs, and given her a child in her old age. Only God could have done it. He will wipe off your tears and take away your rebuke from the surface of the earth. This also is applicable to other challenges of life.

Elizabeth and Zechariah waited and had John. Hannah waited and had Samuel. Mary waited as a virgin and had Jesus Christ, our Lord. Please wait, pray, and trust in the promises of God.

Abraham's Test of Faith

A test of faith is when God asks you to bear what seems unbearable or to do what seems unreasonable before you can receive what seems impossible. A test of faith is about God allowing His elect, like Joseph and Job and other men and women of God, to go through some furnace of affliction in the hands of man and Satan. The test shows whether they are ready to do His will to the end or they will deny Him and backslide.

Abraham went through eight such tests. Sometimes he failed and sometimes he passed, but certainly the sum total of his faithfulness outweighed his failures. He was counted as faithful.

1. *The family test* when he had to leave his family and step out in faith to go to a new land he did not know.
2. *The famine test* which Abraham failed because he doubted God and went down to Egypt.
3. *The fellowship test* when he gave Lot first choice concerning the pasture land.
4. *The fighting test* when he won the victory over the kings of the cities of the plains.
5. *The fortune test* when he refused the wealth of the king of Sodom.
6. *The fatherhood test* which he failed when he agreed to Sarah's plan to have a child with Hagai.
7. *The farewell test* when he said goodbye to his son Ishmael.
8. *The sacrifice test* when he obeyed God's instruction to sacrifice his covenant child, Isaac, at Mount Moriah.

> There can be no conquest without combat, no triumph without trial, no testimony without testing. Your trials will soon turn to uncommon testimonies.

There is always a time difference between when you are called and time of sending out. During this period, you will surely go through trials of faith. You may pass your test or fail it before you can be sent forth.

The Bible says:

Remember how the Lord your God led you all the way in the desert these forty years, to humble you and to test you in order to know what was in your heart, whether or not you would keep his commands. He humbled you, causing you to hunger and then feeding you with manna, which neither you nor your fathers had known, to teach you that man does not live on bread alone but on every word that comes from the mouth of the Lord. (Deut. 8:2–3)

The big question is, how will you know if the problem in your life is a test of faith or a devilish affliction? The answer is that if you have promises of God in your life and are faithfully obedient to His commandments, then you are going through some trial of faith. God will surely see you through. 'Thou therefore endure hardness, as a good soldier of Jesus Christ' (2 Tim. 2:3).

It is sometimes difficult to understand the ways of the Lord, He is the chief Giver, and He expects believers to give all liberally. You can be tested with what you have, like Abraham.

> Any time you obey God, you move a step higher in His glory.

Abraham waited for one hundred years to have his promised child Isaac. Then God demanded that Abraham go to Mount Moriah to offer his only begotten son as sacrifice to Him.

James, a servant of God and of the Lord Jesus Christ, to the twelve tribes which are scattered abroad, greetings. My brethren, count it all joy when ye fall into diverse temptations; Knowing this, that the trying of your faith worketh patience. But let patience have her perfect work, that ye may be perfect and entire, wanting nothing. If any of you lack wisdom, let him ask of God, that giveth to all men liberally, and upbraideth not; and it shall be given him. But let him ask in faith, nothing wavering. For he that wavereth is like a wave of the sea driven with the wind and tossed. (Jas. 1:1–6)

All believers face similar temptations, but not all will experience the same kind of trials of faith from God..

The messianic promise in Genesis 3:15 came into focus in the life story of Abraham. 'Sometime later, God tested Abraham, He said to Him, "Abraham" "here I am" he replied. Then God said, take your son, your only son Isaac whom you love, and go to the region of Moriah. Sacrifice him there on one of the mountains I will tell you about' (Gen. 22:1–2).

God's promise to Abraham carried the messianic sacrifice to conquer the old serpent who tempted and deceived humanity. God was using Abraham's trial of faith to demonstrate what God Himself would do with His only begotten Son on the cross at Calvary,

The tests of faith for Abraham, Joseph, and Job teach that when you pass your test, God's manifold restoration will begin to take place. Often we do not see God at work when we go through tests. Rather, we consider all adversity as afflictions of the Devil or punishment for the sins we have committed.

> You have to see the invisible first for you to do the impossible

What a dreadful command Abraham received from God. He was being asked to give up his pride and joy. Not only that; God was directing him to act contrary to all that He had previously promised. Abraham had dismissed his other son on God's directive. Now he was asked to sacrifice the unique son upon whom all God's promises rested.

How do you stand on the promises of God in your days of testing? Do you lament that God has forsaken you? 'Fear not; I'm with you,' says the Lord. Are you fighting with God in your spirit as you go through your trial of faith, especially when everyone around you is mocking you like Job's friends mocked him? Listen, friend: God is with you till the end of time.

The Bible says:

He will wipe off tears from your eyes, there will be no more death or mourning or crying or pain for the former things has passed away. (Rev. 21:4)

One day, the angels of the Lord came to present themselves before the Lord and Satan also came with them. The Lord said to Satan 'Where have you come from?' Satan answered to the Lord, 'From roaming through the earth and going back and forth of it.' Then the Lord said to Satan, have you considered my servant Job? There is no one on earth like him, he is blameless and upright, a man who fears God and shun evil. (Job. 1:6–8)

The Bible says that Satan descended on Job and destroyed all that belonged to him, including his livestock, his estate, his business, his finances, and his family. Even Job's health was affected.

Trust in the Word and Promises of God

Job and his comforting friends did not know that Job's suffering was a special test of faith in the hands of God. The call to Abraham for him to offer his son Isaac was likewise a divine test. It was quite remarkable how Abraham obeyed so rapidly. Abraham prepared himself for the journey with his son and some servants. When he got to the foot of the mountain, as directed by God, Abraham left the servants with the donkeys at the foot and told them to wait there. 'The lad and I will go yonder and worship and we will come back to you' (Gen. 22:5).

The last stage of the journey was the hardest. The old man had fire and a knife. The young boy carried the wood. They made their journey silently up the mountain. All of a sudden, Isaac broke the silence with a question: 'Look the fire and the wood, but where is the lamb for a burnt offering?' (Gen. 22:7).

Abraham replied to his son with a statement of faith and said, in effect, 'don't worry, son': 'God will provide for Himself the lamb for the burnt offering' (Gen. 22:8).

Abraham and Isaac prepared the sacrificial altar. As Abraham laid his hand on his son to slaughter him, one can only imagine what was running through his mind! However, Abraham remained faithful and obedient to God's command. Abraham prepared his son for the sacrifice.

As his hand was raised to cut Isaac's throat, God intervened: 'But the angel of the Lord called out to him from heaven, "Abraham, Abraham" here I am he replied. Do not lay a hand on the boy, he said "Do not do anything to him, now I know that you fear God because you have not withheld from me your son, you only son. Abraham looked up and there in a thicket, he saw a ram caught by its horns, he went over and took the ram and sacrificed it as a burnt offering instead of his son' (Gen. 22:11–13).

This whole testing experience of Abraham foreshadowed the great sacrifice of the coming seed of the woman on the cross at Calvary for the redemption of believers. Isaac characterised what was prophesied concerning Jesus, the Son of God. As Isaac did not resist his father, so also did Jesus, the Son of God, go like a lamb to the slaughter, become an offering, rise bodily from the dead, and ascend into His glory (Isa. 53:7–12; Acts 8:32–35).

We see in this great test of Abraham the symbolic truth concerning Jesus Christ, the unique begotten Son of God: 'You have not withheld your son, your only son.' Abraham's great faith earned him an everlasting covenant:

The angel of the Lord called to Abraham from heaven a second time and said, I swear by my name declares the Lord, that because you have done this and you have not withheld your son, your only son, I will surely bless you and make your descendants numerous as the stars of the sky and as sand of the seashore.

Your descendants will take possession of the cities of their enemies and through your offspring, all nations on earth will be blessed because you have obeyed me. (Gen. 22:15–18)

Jesus, the Saviour of the world, was an offspring of Abraham, bringing salvation to the entire human race through His death and resurrection.

> Stand faithfully in obedience to the promises of God, no matter how long the delay, He will surely fulfil his promises.

The Bible says, 'Not one of all the good promises the LORD your God gave you has failed. Every promise has been fulfilled; not one has failed' (Josh. 23:14). 'Imitate those who through faith and PATIENCE inherited what had been promised' (Heb. 6:12).

> The Devil will not chase empty vessels. God has a place for you in His kingdom, and you are loaded with the promises of God. Hence the Devil is after you. It takes faithfulness in God to overcome the Wicked One and be fruitful in life. Any time you obey God, you move a step higher in His glory.

The human mind is the most powerful laboratory. There, God has established the creative machine called faith to fabricate things into existence as He does at creation when He created the Heaven and Earth (Genesis 1).

CHAPTER 3

Joseph's Dream Promise

The fascinating story of Joseph, the number-eleven son of Jacob (renamed Israel), has held generations of men and women spellbound. It continues to reveal a fascinating account of how God brought His promises to fulfilment amid human and satanic efforts to thwart those promises.

The trial of faith in the life of Joseph marked the beginning or the partial fulfilment of God's promise to Abraham: that his descendants would be strangers for four hundred years in a land that was not theirs, and that they would eventually return (Gen. 15:13–16). It brought into focus the revelation of how God intended to carry out His work of the redemption of mankind from the captivity of Satan, as promised in Genesis 3:15. It also revealed that God can do anything that is beyond human imagination to protect whoever is bearing His promises. He will faithfully bring His promises to fruition at all cost because He is the Omnipotent, Omniscient and Omnipresent God in Charge of all things.

The Bible account says, 'Joseph a young man of seventeen was tending the flocks with his brother, the sons of Bilhah and the sons of Zilpah, his father's wives, and he brought their father a bad report about them. Now Israel loved Joseph more than any of his other sons, because he had been born to him in his old age; and he made a richly ornamented robe for him' (Gen. 37:2–3).

Joseph was 17 years old when God visited him in night dreams with promises that appeared to be an extension of the covenant promises made to Abraham and confirmed to Isaac and Jacob. Joseph shared the dreams with the household of Jacob, not realizing the consequential effect of his action. His brothers hated him and sold him into slavery, foreshadowing the enslavement of the descendants of Abraham in Egypt for 430 years.

Let us make some reference here to enable us appreciate God's faithfulness in His Word and promises. We know about the period in Joseph's life when he was sold into slavery, as well as the length of time he spent as a slave and prisoner in Egypt before he was elevated by Pharaoh at the age of 30 to fulfil his destiny. Joseph was 39 years old when he revealed himself to his brothers (Gen. 41:1–45:8). He introduced his father Jacob, who was 130 years old, to Pharaoh (Gen. 47:9). This means that Jacob was about ninety when Joseph was born and aged 107 when Joseph was 17.

When the time came for her "Rebecca" to give birth, there were twin boys in her womb the first to come out was red, and his whole body was like a hairy garment; so they named him Esau. After this, his brother came out, with his hand grasping Esau's heel; so he was named Jacob. Isaac was sixty years old when Rebecca gave birth to them. (Gen. 25:24–26)

This informs us that Isaac was sixty when his wife gave birth to Jacob and Isaac. Isaac died when he was aged 180 years:

Isaac lived a hundred and eighty years. Then he breathed his last and was gathered to his people old and full of years. And his sons Esau and Jacob buried him. (Gen. 35:28–29)

This means that Isaac was still alive, as a grandfather aged 167, when Joseph was 17 years and sold into slavery.

Now Israel loved Joseph more than any of his other sons, because he had been born to him in his old age; and he made a richly ornamented robe for him. (Gen. 37:3)

Jacob made to Joseph a very valuable garment to express his love for him. Joseph was the firstborn of his favourite wife, Rachel, who later died giving birth to Benjamin. However, Jacob seems to have learned nothing from his own experience as a child, when his father Isaac chose Esau as his favourite.

Jacob's special treatment of Joseph caused resentment among his sons. 'When the brothers saw that their father loved him more than all his brothers, they hated him' (Gen. 37:4).

Joseph Dreams

Joseph had two special dreams. These dreams were prophetic. Both carried the same promises. They foretold a time when Joseph would be a leader over his people. His brothers understood the message and asked, 'Shall you indeed rule over us?' (Gen. 37:8). The double dreams made fulfilment sure. He would be a messiah of his people, a predecessor of Jesus Christ.

The first dream involved sheaves belonging to his brothers bowing down to Joseph's sheaf. In the second dream, the sun, moon, and eleven stars bowed down to Joseph's star. Although Jacob rebuked Joseph for relating such dreams, he, like Mary, who kept things and pondered them in her heart, kept the matter of the dreams in his mind.

These dreams would have helped Joseph as he was passing through his severe trials.

> If you do not have a dream, you don't have a tomorrow.

While the sons of Leah had a good reason to be jealous of Joseph, the sons of Bilhah and Zilpah had other reasons for despising him. Things went from bad to worse when Joseph told them his dreams: 'They hated him even more' (Gen. 37:5); 'his brethren envied him' (Gen. 37:11).

Joseph was naive and insensitive to have shared his dreams with men who could not tolerate being in his presence. This should be a lesson for others not to share their dreams freely with people around them, lest they become victims just like Joseph.

> Dare to dream. Look at things not as they are but as they should be in future. Creativity is built into every one of us; it is part of our DNA. Dream's second name is *spiritual horsepower.*

The promises of God for Joseph led to a new level of cruelty against him by his brothers: '"Look, this dreamer is coming" then they conspired against him to kill him, and said we shall see what will become of his dream!' (Gen. 37:?).

The Plot against Joseph

As a result of the promises of God to Joseph, which were revealed through his prophetic dreams, his brothers planned to kill him and throw his body in a pit. They lied to their father that 'some wild animals has devoured him', just to prevent the fulfilment of the promises.

> The Devil will never chase an empty vessel. You are loaded with substance; hence the attack. Your saving grace is to trust and be faithful to the almighty God.

Reuben came up with a plan to spare Joseph's life. He advised, 'Shed no blood, but cast him into this pit.' Reuben's plan was to deliver Joseph from the hands of his brothers and bring him back to their father. But the other brothers were so cruel and callous, they turned deaf ears to Reuben's plea for mercy. However, the plan of God for Joseph allowed Reuben's plan to come to fruition.

The sons of Jacob seized Joseph and threw him into a cistern. The Bible says, 'So, when Joseph came to his brothers, they stripped him of his robe – the richly ornamented robe he was wearing and they took him and threw him into the cistern. Now the cistern was empty, there was no water in it' (Gen. 37:23–24). They took Joseph's robe, slaughtered a goat, and dipped the robe in the goat's blood.

The plan of Joseph's brothers at that time was to allow Joseph to get dehydrated in the cistern and die. Judah came up with another idea of selling Joseph to the Midianite traders to make some money so that they would not, by allowing their brother to die in the cistern, be guilty of murder. Judah reminded his brothers, 'He is our brother and our flesh' (Gen. 37:27. They agreed. They pulled Joseph out of the pit and sold him 'for twenty shekels of silver' (Gen. 37:28).

Their action was no less a crime. To sell their brother into slavery was a capital offence. Regrettably, this was the beginning of the enslavement of the children of Israel in a foreign land for 400 years according to God's prophecy to Abraham. 'Then the Lord said to him, know for certain that your descendants will be strangers in a country not their own and they will be enslaved and mistreated four hundred years' (Gen. 15:13).

When the sad news was eventually relayed to Jacob, he was devastated. 'He tore his clothes, put sackcloth on his waist, and mourned for his son for many days' (Gen. 37:34).

I don't know what you're going through in your life as you are reading this book,. You may be facing persecution, afflictions, and other devastating experiences like Joseph and Job. I urge you to take a stock of your relationship with God. Are you a born-again child of God? Do you obey God's commandments? Do you keep your marriage in accordance with your wedding vows? Do you worship your God in spirit and truth? Do you love your neighbour like yourself and get involved in the work of evangelism? Have you forgiven those who have trespassed against you?

If the answer to these questions is yes, I urge you to stand on the promises of God. Whatever you're going through could be a trial of faith like Joseph's. There is light at the end of the tunnel; just trust in His Word and His promises. It is said of our Lord that 'He endured the cross despising the shame because of the joy that was set before him' (Heb. 12:2).

You may be going through fire; He has promised it will not burn you. You may be going through the waters; He has promised they will not overflow you and the land will not swallow you (Isaiah 43:2-3).

It takes faithfulness in God to overcome every obstacle in life. Miracles happen when the level of faith is higher than the level of fear and doubt.

Joseph's Potiphar Trial

Meanwhile, the nomadic Midianite traders sold Joseph in Egypt to Potiphar, an officer of Pharaoh and captain of the guard. At this point, one might well wonder how Joseph's dreams could come to pass. One thing stands sure: God was with Joseph as he was going through those crises and kept him alive. His brothers conspired to destroy the very person ordained by God to bless them and preserve their lives. In a similar way, Jesus's own people plotted to destroy the Messiah ordained to save them and the entire world.

The Bible says that 'the Lord was with Joseph' (Gen. 39:2). God was with Joseph in his troubles and gave him success in adversity.

The hard lesson in Joseph's case is that God did not take Joseph out of adversity just because he was the bearer of God's promises. But God was with him and enabled him to triumph. The Bible says, 'When you pass through the waters, I will be with you, and when you pass through the rivers they will not sweep over you. When you walk through the fire, you will not be burnt; the flame will not set you ablaze' (Isa. 43:2).

Joseph was in favour both with God and with Potiphar, his master. 'So, he left in Joseph's care, everything he had; with Joseph in charge, he did not concern himself with anything except the food he ate. Now Joseph was well-built and handsome' (Gen. 39:6). Suddenly Joseph was confronted with a different test.

Potiphar's wife 'cast longing eyes' and determined to seduce Joseph. Choosing the right moment when no one was around, she boldly accosted Joseph and said to him, 'Lie with me.'

It was a severe temptation, a heart-breaking temptation for the bearer of God's promises, for it was not a slave girl who made the proposal, but his master's wife. 'But he refused, "with me in charge" he told her, "my master does not concern himself with anything in this house, everything he owns he has entrusted to my care, "no one is greater in this house than I am" my master has withheld nothing from me except you, because you are his wife, how then could I do such a wicked thing and sin against God' (Gen. 39:8-9).

His reply exhibited some degree of courage, self-control, and consciousness of the fear of God. Joseph gave three reasons for rejecting Potiphar's wife's advances. To yield to this temptation would mean betraying trust, damaging a marriage, and sinning against God.

> There is little that can withstand a man who can conquer himself. The only giant who can stop you from possessing your Promised Land is yourself. 'He that hath no rule over his own spirit is like a city that is broken down, and without walls' (Prov. 25:28).

It is a great temptation for a young, virile, single man to have sex with his boss's wife, and the temptation occurred day after day. Not only did Joseph refuse to go to bed with her, he also tried to avoid being with her.

The first refusal helped Joseph to say no to every subsequent temptation until the final onslaught. Potiphar's wife was a determined woman who always had her way. The opportunity she had been waiting for came when |Joseph was in the house alone: 'One day he went into the house to attend to his duties, and none of the household servants was inside. She caught him by his cloak and said; "come to bed with me" but he left his cloak in her hand and ran out of the house' (Gen. 39:11–12).

Temptation of this kind needs to be dealt with in a radical way. The commandment is to flee from sexual immorality (1 Cor. 6:18). As Potiphar's wife grabbed Joseph hoping that her touch would break down his resolve, Joseph sensed danger and broke free.

> The amount of truth you know determines the degree of freedom you'll experience. (See John 8:32.)

The woman felt humiliated by Joseph's refusal and took her revenge. She lied when she reported the incident to her husband.

She kept his cloak beside her until his master came home. Then she told him this story; "That Hebrew slave you brought us came to me to make sport of me. But as soon as I screamed for help, he left his cloak beside me and ran out of the house." (Gen. 39:16–18)

She painted a picture of her own innocence. 'In the war between falsehood and truth, falsehood wins the first battle, but truth wins the war.'

When the master heard the story his wife told him saying, this is how slave treated me. He burned with anger. Joseph's master took him and put him in prison, the place where the king's prisoners were confined. And Joseph was there in the prison. (Gen. 39:19–20)

Joseph Imprisoned

What a devastating and horrible experience for a teenage boy. What was going on in Joseph's mind? What gave him the courage to face all his challenges without going into depression?

> There can be no conquest without combat, no triumph without trial, and no testimony without testing. 'Thou therefore endure hardness, as a good soldier of Jesus Christ' (2 Tim. 2:3).

History seemed to be repeating itself for Joseph. For the second time he had been taken prisoner for his faithfulness, and his clothing had been used to make a false report against him.

Let's ask this golden question: why would God allow His servant, who carried the promise to lead his people, to be treated unjustly even when he had sought to do what was right? When and how would the promise of leadership come to fruition in the life of a slave-turned-prisoner in a foreign land?

Only God could give the answer.

> If you do not have a dream, you don't have a tomorrow. Success is about going from failure to failure without losing enthusiasm. The dream-promise of God for Joseph kept him gazing at his tomorrow in his adversity.

Joseph was spiritually alive and remained focused on the promises of God. I urge you, beloved, to remain focused on the promised dream of God for your tomorrow, not who you are or the circumstances in your life today. The more you look back, the less you get ahead into your tomorrow. No man is rich enough to buy his past. So, stand on the promises of God.

The Bible says, 'The Lord was with him, He showed him mercy and granted him favour in the eyes of the prison warden' (Gen. 39:21). God's grace was with Joseph in the disasters of his being sold into slavery and his imprisonment on false charges. God was working with Joseph to change all the disastrous circumstances in his life to blessings and victory.

> Remember that a man is not finished when he is defeated; he is finished when he quits. In trials, too many people quit trying, but accomplishers stand during trials and succeed. "For a just man falleth seven times, and riseth up again: but the wicked must fall into mischief' (Prov. 24:16a).

Joseph foreshadowed the experience of his descendants, who became slaves in Egypt. God was with them, as He was with Joseph, and led them out in fulfilment of his promises.

Joseph also points us to Jesus Christ, the Son of God, the suffering Servant who was treated as the worst criminal. 'Yet, it was the Lord's will to crush him and cause him to suffer, and through the Lord makes his life a guilt offering, he will see his offspring and prolong his days, and the will of the Lord will prosper in his hand' (Isa. 53:10).

God was with Joseph in the prison and showed him mercy and covenant love. God gave him favour in the sight of the prison warden, and it was not long before Joseph was given responsibility and authority in the prison. The Bible says that the prison governor committed to Joseph's hand all the prisoners who were in the prison. Because God was with him, he was successful. This also confirmed that God was preparing him for the fulfilment of his dream promise.

Have you been being treated unfairly by people around you and wondered whether life is really worth living? Does your life mirror the life of Joseph? Let Joseph's experience and the way he maintained faithfulness with God under severe circumstances and pressure be an inspiration to you. God was with Joseph in all of his adversities and gave him success,. The Lord did not take Joseph out of the troubles, but He enabled him to triumph in adversity. This must be a big lesson for you as you're going through your trial.

God has not promised any man an easy ride to the Promised Land, but He has promised that 'when you pass through the waters, I will be with you, when you pass through the waters they will not sweep over you. When you walk through the fire, you will not be burned; the flames will not set you ablaze' (Isa. 43:2).

Does your life mirror the life of Joseph even after God promised to bless and prosper you? Not to worry; your success has less to do with speed and more to do with divine direction and timing. It takes a new mind to mind the things of God. 'Let this mind be in you, which was also in Christ Jesus' (Phil. 2:5).

If you can understand the timing of God, then you can move into the things of God,. There is little that can withstand a man who can conquer himself,. How you react to crisis displays your level of maturity in faith, which determines your destiny. Joseph displayed excellent faith in his trials, and God elevated him to fulfil all His promises. Don't be afraid of changes. Change is an unchangeable law of progress and success.

Joseph was conscious of God's anointing upon his life. He trusted in the faithfulness of God, who promised even as circumstances suggested impossibility. Joseph believed that every effort of man to thwart the promises of God would fail, so he remained focused on his tomorrow. The Bible says, 'I consider that our present suffering are not worth comparing with the glory that will be revealed in us' (CITATION). This was the rock upon which Joseph stood. He was confident that the picture of God's glory that had been revealed to him in his promise dream would surely come to pass. 'Being fully persuaded that God had power to do what he had promised' (Rom. 8:18).

Have you lost hope? Do you think it is over? Just gird yourself with faith, holiness, truth, love, and forgiveness, then be expectant. His visitation will come when you least expect it. What appear to be evil and disastrous events in your life may turn out to be God's leadership drive to bring His promises to fruition. He may want to use what people see as disaster, to accomplish those promises He made years ago.

God has many ways of making Himself known to man. In the seemingly hopeless case of Joseph, the sovereign God of all life spoke to Pharaoh through his dreams, which none among the magicians, sorcerers and wise men of Egypt could interpret. God had divinely prepared Joseph to unveil their meaning so that His promises could be fulfilled.

Prison to Prominence

Many years before, Joseph's dreams led his brothers to mockingly call him 'the dreamer' and subsequently sell him into slavery (Gen. 37:19, 28). Now the dreams of Pharaoh's officials and particularly of Pharaoh himself were the instruments used by God to fulfil His promises in the life of Joseph. The story of Joseph rising from being in prison for his refusal to sin against God to a place of prominence in Egypt confirmed that 'with God all things are possible' (Gen. 39:9). 'The seemingly bad experiences of life as well as those experiences that we like are all working together for good for those who love God and who are called according to His purpose' (Rom. 8:28).

When you think it is over and that God has forsaken you, understand that God is very much in control of your situation and circumstances. God never makes mistakes. He works out things according to His eternal plans.

Pharaoh's Dreams

Pharaoh's dreams occurred at the time of his birthday, about two years after his cup-bearer had been released from prison. In the first dream, Pharaoh found himself standing by the river. Seven well-fed cows came out of the water and grazed in the meadow. This symbolised Egypt's fertility. These seven cows were closely followed by another seven thin and ugly-looking cows, which ate up the seven fat cows.

Pharaoh woke up from this terrible nightmare but soon fell asleep again and found himself in another dream. This time he saw seven plump heads of grain on one stalk suddenly appear. Up sprang seven thin heads, blighted and withered by the east wind from the desert, and again the thin devoured the fat (Gen. 41:1–7).

When Pharaoh again, he was troubled in his spirit. He knew these dreams were a great revelation and quickly called those who were skilled in the interpretation of dreams in Egypt – the magicians, the star-gazers, the sorcerers, and so on. None could interpret the dreams.

The way Joseph conducted himself in prison and correctly interpreted the dreams of former royal prisoners contributed to his spectacular rise to power. 'Those who succeed are those who forge on when they fail. But those who fail are those who do nothing when they fail'.

Dare to dream. Look at things not as they are, but as they should be according to God's promise. Miracles happen when the level of faith is higher than the level of fear and doubt. You'll surely arrive at your Promised Land. Let your faith in God's promises be your navigator as you journey through the wilderness of your trials. God never fails.

This true story of Joseph rising from slavery to prison to palace encourages us to believe that what we call miracles are all in God's plan. Situations can make us discouraged when we look at life's trials from the human angle, but the life of Joseph encourages us to look higher. The trial you are going through could be God's ways of training and preparing you for greater challenges.

When the royal cup-bearer heard of Pharaoh's dreams and the failure of the magicians to interpret them, he recalled his encounter with Joseph in the prison. He explained to Pharaoh how a young Hebrew man had correctly interpreted his dream.

At this moment, Joseph became the interpreter of dreams which Pharaoh desperately needed, thus setting the stage for Joseph to move from a state of humiliation to an exalted position. Pharaoh had no option but to call for Joseph because his own diviners had let him down. He was desperate to find the correct interpretation to his dreams.

> God often brings people to the end of themselves by cutting off all aids and comfort so that they will turn in humility to the Lord.

Joseph was released from the prison, and the garment of rejection and limitation was removed from him. He was clothed in the garment of honour and praise and summoned to stand before Pharaoh.

Pharaoh explained the reason why Joseph was suddenly called to the palace: 'Pharaoh said to Joseph, and no one can interpret it but I have heard it said that when you hear a dream you can interpret it' (Gen. 41:15).

Joseph, however, quickly ascribed all wisdom, knowledge, understanding, and glory to God: '"I cannot do it" Joseph replied to Pharaoh, but God will give Pharaoh the answer he desires' (Gen. 41:16). Pharaoh proceeded to narrate his dreams to Joseph (Gen. 41:17–24).

As Joseph interpreted the symbolic nature of the dream, twice he testified of the true God to the king of Egypt: 'God has shown Pharaoh what he is about to do' (Gen. 41:25, 28). Joseph brought the interpretation to a close by making double reference to God: 'The reason the dream was given to Pharaoh in two forms is that the matter has been firmly decided by God and God will do it soon' (Gen. 41:32).

Joseph was not a fortune teller, but he was a spokesman for God. He realised that God had revealed all these things for a purpose, and that God had not revealed all these things to Pharaoh for him to just nod his head and brush them aside without a solution. Thus, Joseph advised the king as to what action he should take. He suggested that a qualified person should be appointed to be the controller-general of the food supply in Egypt, a person with 'discerning ability and wise'. Joseph also recommended that Pharaoh appoint other officers to oversee the food conservation programme, and suggested that a fifth of each harvest should be stored yearly for seven years in order to carry them through the years of famine.

Joseph Becomes Prime Minister

The dream promise of God for Joseph was established when he was 17 years old. The journey toward fulfilment had taken Joseph through cistern, slavery, prison, and palace. Now Pharaoh's dreams became the instrument used by God to bring His promise dream to Joseph to fulfilment at the age of 30.

> Our success has less to do with our speed and ability but more to do with God's direction and timing. (See Eccl. 3:11.)

Perhaps, you have lost hope and concluded that God has forgotten and has forsaken you? No. God is at work, He's not finished yet. Remember that it took twenty-five years for Abraham to see the birth of his promised child Isaac. It took over thirteen years for David to ascend the throne as king of Israel after he was anointed in Ramah at the age of 17. Every person called by God must have their moment of refinement before fulfilment. Therefore focus on the promises of God as you are going through your period of refining.

In one day, God wiped the tears from the eyes of Joseph, the son of Jacob and the promised leader of His people Israel. Joseph was exalted to the office of prime minister of Egypt (Gen. 41:43). 'Then Pharaoh said to Joseph, I am Pharaoh but without your word, no one will lift hand or foot in all Egypt. Pharaoh gave the name Zaphenath-Paneah and gave him Asehath daughter of Potiphera, priest of On. To be his wife. And Joseph went throughout the land of Egypt' (Gen. 41:44–45).

Only God has the final say. I challenge you to challenge your God with your faith now. Your faith is crucial to your rising into God's glory. In your trying time, without faith, you cannot please God.

Joseph was faithful and dependent on God for wisdom. He was given dominion over all the land of Egypt (Gen. 41:41, 43–46).

Joseph's Dream Fulfilled

Joseph interpreted Pharaoh's dream and was exalted to the highest office in Egypt. However, what about his own dream to be leader of his people?

At the time of Joseph's miraculous rise, Jacob his father, his ten brothers, his sisters, and the wives of his brothers were still alive in Canaan, now plagued with famine. (I am sure that Potiphar and his wife were still alive too.) In thirteen years, Jacob had never stopped grieving for Joseph. Likewise, Joseph's older brothers had never forgotten the evil they did in selling Joseph as slave to the Midianites.

The famine in the land of Canaan hit hard on Jacob's family and made the household of Jacob look beyond Canaan for a solution. God was using this famine to bring Jacob's family together again and prepare them for the great exodus. When Jacob heard that there was grain in Egypt, he decided not to move his family to Egypt, as had his grandfather Abraham and his father Isaac. Instead, he sent his sons to Egypt to buy grain (Gen. 42:1).

All ten of Joseph's brothers agreed to go to Egypt. But in God's programme, it was a journey to fulfil the will of God concerning the promise dream He made to Joseph. So Benjamin, the last son, was kept at home with Jacob.

Jacob's older sons embarked on their journey to Egypt and arrived safely. It happened that they found themselves in the presence of the prime minister and not any Egyptian officer appointed to sell grain. According to the custom of the land – coupled with the programme of God for Jacob's household – they all bowed. 'When Joseph's brothers arrived, they bowed down to him with their faces to the ground' (Gen. 42:6).

What an incredible experience orchestrated by our awesome and omnipotent God, who is able to bring all impossibility to possibility. He is the Alpha and the Omega, the beginning and the end of all things. The Bible says, 'The fools says in their hearts, there is no God. They are corrupt, their deeds are vile, there is no one who does good' (Ps. 14:1).

The sons of Jacob thought in their hearts that they had succeeded in thwarting the plan of God for Joseph. Little did they know that they were tools in the hand of God and were working for God to actualise His promise for Joseph.

Your enemies are like them. Your enemies are coming back to bow down before you,. Remember, as I said earlier, you are a victim in the hands of the Devil because of the substance in you. But God's business never fails. Whatever He has ordained will surely come to pass. He must surely bring his plan to fruition.

The Bible says:

Say to him, be careful, keep calm and don't be afraid. Do not lose heart because of these two smouldering stubs of firewood because of the fierce anger of Rezin and Aram and of the son of Remaliah, Aran, Ephraim and Ramaliah's son have plotted your ruin saying, let us invade Judah; let us tear it apart and divide it among ourselves, and make the son of Tabeel king over it. Yet this is what the Sovereign Lord says 'it will not take place, it will not happen'. (Isa. 7:4–7)

Beloved, verily, God is alive forever and able to save all who trust and obey Him. He is prepared to do anything to bring His promises to fulfilment. He is equally prepared to deal ruthlessly with all His enemies who contend with His authority. Believe, obey, and trust. You will see the glory of God.

Joseph instantly remembered his promise dreams about his brothers (Gen. 42:9). But they could not recognise him because Joseph was the last person they expected to see. Joseph decided to act strangely to them and speak roughly (Gen. 42:7)

During this wonderful experience, Joseph could hardly control his emotions. Judah's moving words were the last straw. After ordering his Egyptian attendants out of the room Joseph wept aloud in the presence of his brothers.

Trust in the Word and Promises of God

And Joseph said to his brothers, I am Joseph! Is my father still living? But his brothers were not able to answer him, because they were terrified at his presence. Then Joseph said to his brothers, come close to me. When they had done so, he said, I am your brother Joseph the one you sold into Egypt. And now, do not be distressed and do not be angry with yourselves for selling me here, because it was to save lives that God sent me ahead of you. For two years now, there had been famine and for the next five years there will not be ploughing and reaping but God sent me ahead of you to preserve for you a remnant on earth and to save your lives by a great deliverance. So then, it was not you who sent me here, but God. He made me father to Pharaoh, lord of his entire household and ruler of all Egypt. (Gen. 45:3–8)

I prophesy into your life that as you are reading this book, you will encounter a miracle, a supernatural breakthrough that will cause all your enemies to be terrified in your presence. You will also be a means of sustenance for your enemies from henceforth in the name of Jesus Christ. Just say a louder amen.

Joseph made frantic efforts to calm the fears of his brothers. He told them that their wicked actions, for which they were now truly repentant, had been used by God to preserve life. God sent me before you to preserve lives (Gen. 45:5). God sent me before you to preserve posterity for you in the earth (Gen. 45:7). So now it was not you that sent me here but God (Gen. 45:8). God has made me lord of all Egypt (Gen. 45:9).

It may look impossible, but your days of visitation and uncommon testimonies are around the corner. Keep thanking, praising, and worshipping your God for what He will soon do in your life. 'Through these he has given us his very great and precious promises. So that through them you may participate in the divine nature and escape the corruption in the world caused by evil desires' (2 Pet. 1:4).

Joseph Foreshadows the Coming of Jesus Christ, the Messiah

Joseph	Christ
Joseph was rejected by his own brothers (Gen. 37:19–20), stripped of his robe, and thrown into a pit (Gen. 37:22–24). Sold into slavery, he eventually landed in a dungeon in Egypt (Gen. 37:28; 39:20).	Christ was rejected by his own (John 1:11). He was stripped of his robe, condemned to death and descended to hell (Matt. 27:27–31; John 19:23–24; 1 Pet. 3:18–20).
Joseph was an exemplary servant (Gen. 39:13–20). Though he was tempted, he did not give in to temptation (Gen. 39:7–12).	Christ came as a servant (Phil. 2:7). He was tempted, but did not sin (Heb. 4:15).
Joseph was unjustly accused and condemned (Gen. 39:13–20). In prison, Joseph interpreted a dream of life to one of his fellow prisoners and death to another (Gen. 40:6–23). He was raised out of the dungeon to sit at Pharaoh's right hand (Gen. 41:14–45).	Christ was unjustly accused and condemned (Matt. 26:57–68; 27:11–25). While on the cross, Jesus's words promised life to one of the thieves condemned with him (Luke 23:39–43). Jesus was raised from the prison of death to sit at the right hand of God the Father (Acts 2:33; 5:31).

Joseph had a meal with his brothers before he revealed himself to them (Gen. 43:16). When he did reveal himself, Joseph saved his brothers' lives (Gen. 45:3–15). Joseph's actions also saved Egypt and many others (Gen. 50:20).	Jesus had a last supper with his disciples (Matt. 26:17–30). After his death and resurrection he revealed himself to them alive, which brought about salvation for them and the world (Luke 24; 1 Cor. 15:1–11).
In Joseph, God partially fulfilled his promise to Abraham to bless all the nations of the world (Gen. 12:1–3), since Joseph's actions helped the nations of the world survive the terrible famine (Gen. 41:57)	In Christ, God completely fulfilled His promise to Abraham (Gen.12:1–3), since Christ died for the sins of the world, and Jesus commanded, "Go and make disciples of all nations" (Matt. 28:19).

Joseph and Jesus were abused, betrayed, and maltreated, yet they were blessings even to those who hurt them. How does this apply to your life as you are going through your own trial? If Jesus can be led to the desert by the Spirit of God to be tempted by Satan, God can also allow you to be tempted.

After the difficult period, God gave Joseph the grace of testimonies. He named his two sons Manasseh, meaning 'God had made me to forget the affliction from my father's household', and Ephraim, meaning 'God had made me to bear fruit in the land of my affliction'.

Be expectant of uncommon testimonies at the end of your afflictions. I decree and declare an uncommon supernatural breakthrough for you as you read through this book in Jesus's name. Amen.

Job's Trials of Faith

Although, the scriptural account of Job does not recount any of God's promises before his trial – he was only referred to as a wealthy man – his test case is a rock-solid reference to strengthen the believer's faith during trials and persecution at the hand of the Devil and his cohorts.

Job's situation indicated that he was a righteous person, blessed by God with the ideal family, 'seven sons and three daughters' (Job 1:2). Job was rich in landed properties, livestock, servants, and possessions, including social standing. He also observed all religious practices. God said that Job was a good person (Job 1:8). But Satan doubted the sincerity of Job and questioned, 'Does Job fear God for nothing?' (Job. 1:9).

God decided to put His reputation on the line. He gave Satan the go-ahead to test Job's faith and see if Job would continue to trust Him. Our faithful fellowship with God during our trial, like that of Job, is crucial. Our trust and faith in God, who is faithful to His Word, is ultimately required to salvage us from the hands of the Devil each time he attacks.

Satan did not spare his sledgehammer against Job; he dealt cruelly with him. While Job's life was in serious peril, his wife mocked him: 'Are you still holding on to your integrity? Curse God and die!' (Job. 2:9).

Job rebuked his wife: 'You are talking like a foolish woman, shall we accept good from God and not trouble' (2:10).

Job's friends were even more cruel in their utterances. They argued that Job was been punished for his sins, adding that he deserved the tragedy in his life. In his response, Job did what seems impossible. He was struggling between the bitter experiences of his losses and the mocking utterances of friends and family. He kept affirming his faith and belief in a loving and fair God, even when all the evidence in his life pointed against God.

For most of the time among his friends, Job sat on the defendant's chair, listening to their negative remarks. Though what his friends were saying seemed right, deep inside his heart, Job knew they were wrong. He looked at his situation from a different angle and explained, 'Then I would still have this consolation … my joy in unrelenting pain that I had not denied the words of the Holy One' (Job 6:10).

Beloved, notwithstanding the challenges in your life presently, let's learn from the trial of Job. Consider his faithfulness to God even when the situation around him seemed hopeless. At a time when life became meaningless for Job, when everything turned negative and everyone around him suggested death, he kept affirming the faithfulness and righteousness of God. He declared, 'Naked came I out of my mother's womb and naked shall I return thither, the Lord gave and the Lord hath taken away, blessed be the name of the Lord' (Job. 1:21). These words are added in the narration: 'In all this Job sinned not, nor charged God foolishly' (v. 22).

Job's faith must have been strengthened with the Word of God in the Scriptures, which says, 'I formed the light and create darkness, I bring prosperity and create disaster, I the Lord do all these things' (Isa. 45:7). This Word became the driven force in Job and developed his heart of praise and worship of God in his anguish. Job asked this pertinent question: 'Shall we accept good from God and not trouble?' (Job 2:10).

Friends, how are you exercising your faith now that all things have turned negative, regardless of the promises of God for your life? Do you still consider God as a faithful and loving God, or as an unfaithful God who is only good when it is good for you? God needs you to praise and worship Him even when things are working in the opposite direction.

God desires that you forgive those who reviled, mocked, spited, and persecuted you, in order for you to receive your own forgiveness and cross to the other side of the river. God inhabits the midst of the praises of His people.

The Devil is simply targeting your faith any time he strikes to afflict you. What he wants ultimately is for you to renounce and forsake God. Once he succeeds in destroying your faith, he will work on you to make you one of his disciples. Your faith is the only vehicle you need to convey you to the land of grace – your Promised Land. Without faith, you cannot please God.

Job perfectly understood this divine principle and applied it to defeat Satan and his cohorts. The Bible says, 'Submit yourself then to God, resist the Devil and he will flee from you' (Jas. 4:7). 'In other that Satan might not outwit us, for we are not unaware of his devices' (2 Cor. 2:11).

The Devil will use your relatives, friends, and acquaintances to get at you – like your husband, wife, siblings, cousins, nephews, colleagues, business partners and neighbours. The Bible says, 'Be vigilant.' Let your faith fight the battle for you.

A trial is a divine school to test your faith and make you complete in the Lord. You come out stronger, better, and more amiable if you allow your faith to be alive during your adversities. God is the Chancellor of the school of faith, Jesus Christ is the Vice-Chancellor, and the Holy Spirit is the Professor. What the Devil does is use those who are closer to you to enforce his evil agenda. What God does is allow the test and go along with you while you are going through the ordeal, as he did with Daniel, Shedrack, Meshack, and Abednego. He will gently embrace you while asking, 'What have you learned from this experiences?'

Thus, with God, our faith grows out of our testing. The Bible says, 'Do not put your trust in princes, in whom there is no help. Happy is he whose hope is in the Lord his God' (Ps. 146:3, 5).

Restoration of Job

Job's trials reached an end. His restoration was essential to silence the Devil, who had been proved totally wrong in his argument with God over Job's faith and God's integrity.

Job also defeated his three friends and his wife, hired by the Devil to persistently rebuke and mock him during his anguish. After God proved the faithfulness of Job, He turned His attention and wrath towards the three friends and asked Job to pray for them in their own affliction. This is how God fights our enemies. The Bible says, 'Then Job replied to the Lord: I know that you can do all things; no plan of your can be thwarted' (Job 42:1–2). This is the foundation and driving force in Job's faith. Job's restoration began with his trust in God and ability to forgive.

After he forgave and prayed for his three friends who had dealt cruelly with him during his anguish, he was wonderfully restored: 'After Job had prayed for his friends, the Lord made him prosperous again and gave him twice as much as he had before' (Job 42:10).

Forgiveness itself is a wonderful experience, a vital tool to disarm and defeat satanic manipulations and destroy seeds of discord. Forgiveness guarantees restoration, rekindles love, and helps to actualise dreams. Forgiveness is also required for anyone to receive forgiveness from God (Matt. 6:14–15). Job had this truth engrafted in his heart and acted accordingly. Ultimately, he never made any charges against God.

Friends, Jesus Christ commands thus: 'You have heard that it was said "love your neighbour and hate your enemies" (Law of Moses) But I (Jesus) tell you, love your enemies and pray for those who persecute you' (Matt. 5:43–44). You need to borrow from Job's experiences in your days of adversity and stop blaming yourself, God, or your foes. Forgive yourself and everyone responsible for your trials and be restored. God has already forgiven you through the death and resurrection of His Son. 'See, I have refined you, though not as silver; I have tested you in the furnace of affliction. For my own sake, for my own sake I have done thing. How can I let myself be defamed? I will not yield my glory to another' (Isa. 48:10).

Prompt your living faith and God will prompt His grace to do the miraculous in your life. Trust God's Word and covenant promises and be glorified in Him.

CHAPTER 4

Davidic Covenant

God's programme of salvation for humanity **and** His incomprehensible love for mankind led to the established covenant promises with Abraham, confirmed to Isaac and Jacob and finally to David, then manifested in our Lord Jesus Christ.

God established that both tradition and political leadership should be subjected to the priestly office and to the sovereign authority of the Most High God. The fascinating story of the anointing of David as king of Israel, in preference to his outwardly more qualified and preferred brothers, strengthens my faith.

David was the least among the sons of Jesse. Actually, he was not considered fit for any meaningful responsibility by his parent. He worked as an errand boy and shepherd boy, tending the flocks. However, God had different purpose for him.

King Saul began to get involved in acts of disobedience to God's instructions and did things to please himself at the peak of his reign in Israel. Saul was anointed to be king and not as a priest, yet he flagrantly abused the authority given to him as king and performed priestly duty. He was sternly rebuked by the prophet Samuel. "'You acted foolishly" Samuel said. "You have not kept the command the Lord your God gave you; if you had, he would have established your kingdom over Israel for all time. But now your kingdom will not endure; the Lord has sought out a man after his heart and appointed him leader of His people, because you have not kept the Lord's command' (1 Sam. 13:13–14).

Subsequently, God rejected Saul as king over Israel because Saul disobeyed His command. God raised His judgement against him through the prophet Samuel: "'You have rejected the word of the Lord, and the Lord has rejected you as king over Israel". As Samuel turned to leave, Saul caught hold of the hem of his robe and it tore. Samuel said to him. The Lord has torn the kingdom of Israel from you today and has given it to one of your neighbours. To one better than you' (1 Sam. 15:26–28).

The Bible says, 'To obey is better than sacrifices and to heed is better than the fat of rams.' Human acts of disobedience to God often stand against the fulfilment of God's promises. Any worship that is not accompanied by obedience is worthless to any individual believer, and it is an insult to God. It is nothing more than rebellion and arrogance. Obedience to God is an indispensable part of true worship.

David Anointed

After the rejection of King Saul, God continued to honour the desires of the Israelites for royal rulership instead of His theocratic rulership. Therefore, God commissioned Samuel to anoint a king for Israel from within the household of Jesse in Bethlehem. The Lord said to Samuel, "How long will you mourn for Saul, since I have rejected him as king over Israel? Fill your horn with oil and be on your way; I am sending you to Jesse of Bethlehem. I have chosen one of his sons to be king' (1 Sam. 16:1). Samuel went as commanded.

Men preferred David's older brothers because they were physically impressive and made attractive candidates for the office of king. But human beings only judge candidates by their outward appearance.

God is the only one who is qualified to choose because God looks at the heart. Man's physical appearance may attract attention, but the quality of a man is on the inside.

'Jesse had seven of his sons pass before Samuel but Samuel said to him the Lord has not chosen these' (1 Sam. 16:10). Humanly speaking, it is certain that Samuel himself would have been wondering and confused by God's rejection of all the seven. Still, Samuel asked Jesse, "'Are these all the sons you have?" "There is still the youngest," Jesse answered. But he is tending the sheep." Samuel said, "Send for him; we will not sit down until he arrives'" (1 Sam. 16:10-11).

The prompt directive that David be brought home suggested to Jesse that his youngest son would be ordained as king. David was rushed home. 'So, he "Jesse" sent and had him "David" brought in, He was ruddy, with a fine appearance and handsome features. Then the Lord said. "Rise and anoint him; he is the one. So Samuel took the horn of oil and anointed him "David" in the presence of his brothers, and from that day on the Spirit of the Lord came upon David in power. Samuel then went to Ramah' (1 Sam. 16:12-13).

Though David had been anointed and the presence, mercy, and favour of God rested upon him, there were still many rivers to cross and many mountains to climb. The challenges ahead of David on his way to the palace were enormous. Goliath was yet to be slain as he would stand roaring, frightening the Israelites and mocking the God of Israel. Saul would become jealous of David and seek to kill him. Many more enemies would be encountered before he finally got to the palace.

As I said earlier, if you are a chosen vessel of God, be prepared for battles. The Devil will not rest and allow you to wage war against his kingdom. He will rise up in war against you. God may not avert wars or troubles, but He promises that He will not forsake you. He will surely lead you through the storms of your life to give you victory over all your enemies.

This is the refining process by which God equips His elect. You cannot surrender or retreat from the battle of the Lord because 'whoever lays hold on the instrument of the kingdom of God and looks back and be fit for the kingdom of God' (Luke 9:62).

God had prepared all those battles for David to fight and to conquer. God was very much aware of those battles, yet God did not avert them for David. He allowed David to face all the battles as a process of refining him for great leadership when he eventually ascended the throne. David must neither surrender nor retreat because God was his shepherd. 'The Lord is my light and my salvation, whom shall I fear? The Lord is the stronghold of my life of whom shall I be afraid? When evil men advance against me to devour my flesh, when my enemies and my foes attack me, they will stumble and fall. Though an army besiege me, my heart will not fear, though war break out against me, even then will I be confident' (Ps. 27:1–3).

Trust in the Word and Promises of God

Joseph was the eleventh son of Jacob, whose call to leadership over the Israelites marked the beginning of a series of battles that led him through the pit to slavery, imprisonment, and finally the palace. Similarly, the anointing of David as king over Israel marked the beginning of his battles with Goliath, Saul, and the Philistines until he finally arrived at the palace as king.

David armed himself with Psalm 23 as a weapon with which to face all the battles of his life. David was conscious of the presence of God with him in every battle he faced and resolved to establish a temple of praise and worship for the Lord. 'After the king had settled in his palace and the Lord had given him rest from all his enemies around him, He "David" said to Nathan the Prophet. "Here I am living in a palace of cedar, while the Ark of God remains in a tent"' (2 Sam. 7:1–2).

Beloved, whatever the promises God has for your life and whatever battles you are facing presently, I know that the victory demands that you turn the temple of your heart to a place of praise and worship, just like David. Trust and believe in Him who promised that He is able. Be faithful to His commands, and He will surely fulfil His promises. 'If you fully obey the Lord your God and carefully follow all His commands I give you today, the Lord your God will set you high above all the nations on earth. All these blessings will come upon you and accompany you if you obey the Lord your God' (Deut. 28:1–2).

Do not focus on or consider the darkness in the tunnel. Focus on the light at the end of the tunnel. You are almost there. Do not rely on your own ability. The selection of David as king of Israel, coupled with his victories over all the battles of his life, pointed to God's faithfulness in fulfilling His promises.

Now then, tell my servant David, this is what the Lord Almighty says ... 'I took you from the pasture and from following the flock to be ruler over my people Israel. I have been with you wherever you have gone, and I have cut off all your enemies from before you. Now I will make your name great like the names of the greatest men of the earth. And I will provide a place for my people Israel and will plant them so that they can have a home of their own and no longer be disturbed. Wicked people will not oppress them anymore, as they did at the beginning and have done ever since the time I appointed leaders over my people Israel. I will give you rest from all your enemies.' (2 Kgs 7:8–11)

God demonstrated His covenant promises to Abraham. They were confirmed to Isaac and Jacob and invested in the life stories of Joseph and David as an everlasting covenant. God promised to bless David and his house forever and to make his name great like the greatest men of the earth, culminating in the manifestation of our Lord Jesus Christ, the Saviour of the world, coming through the lineage of David (Matt. 1:1).

Jesus, our Saviour, also fought His own battles from birth to His crucifixion on the cross, obtaining victory for mankind before He rose from the dead and ascended into His glory. If you are a member of God's covenant promises, you can't be left out. Your victory is certain.

Have you asked this amazing question? Why would God allow Joseph to be thrown into the cistern, sold into slavery and sent to prison before the miracle? After all, God called Joseph. Have you ever wondered why God allowed Daniel to be thrown into the lion's den before rescuing him? Have you ever asked why God stood aloof and watched Shedrack, Meshack, and

Abednego get thrown into the furnace before rescuing them? Have you reflected on why David, who was called from the shepherd's bush at the age of 17 to become king over Israel, would have to fight so many battles before he finally ascended the throne? Have you asked why Jesus Christ would refuse to come to prevent the death of Lazarus, instead waiting for Lazarus to die and decay before finally coming to raise him from death? Your case may be one of such testimonies.

Friend, don't expect to stroll into your Promised Land when Goliath is still bullying, Pharaoh still pursuing, Saul still raging with envy, Delilah and Potiphar's wife still dangling the carrot, and the Devil still going up and down tempting. Be strong in the Lord for the battles. Be courageous, fear not, and be prepared to face the challenges with fasting and prayers. 'For we wrestle not against flesh and blood, but against principalities, against powers, against the rulers of the darkness of this world, against spiritual wickedness in high places' (Eph. 6:12). God is with you. Trust in God's Word and promises and see wonders. 'Consider it pure joy, my brothers, whenever you face trials of many kinds, because you know that the testing of your faith develops perseverance. Persecution must finish its work so that you may be mature and complete, not lacking anything' (Jas. 1:2–4).

Differences between Trial, Persecution, Punishment, and Affliction

There is a need for you to understand the differences between trial, persecution, punishment, and affliction of the Devil.

Trial is a test of faith. It is limited to anointed men and women of destiny with God. Persecution is the conspiracy of evil and wicked people against the anointed men and women of God, such as was done by the elders of the temple against Jesus Christ.

Trial is a process of refinement and training for the chosen men and women of God to become soldiers of Christ, to prepare for the work of the ministry and fight against the kingdom of darkness. Most assuredly, God's presence is always with His anointed ones as they go through their trials and persecutions. He will always lead them through the fire, but the fire will not burn them, and through the waters, but the water will not overflow them (Isa. 43:2). God will always shepherd his chosen ones in the wilderness to protect them from being devoured by the wild beast.

If your level of faith and trust in the Lord during your trials is questionable, that means you cannot be trusted for the things of the kingdom of God. But if your faith and trust in God is solid and unwavering, then He will release His heavy anointing upon your life to break every yoke and remove all burdens (Isa. 10:27).

Punishment and affliction are the lot of disobedient children of God. They occur when God's presence disappears from a person's life. Then the Devil's presence becomes visible and begins to afflict the person with all manner of sickness, disease, poverty, failure, disappointment, setback, limitation, stagnancy, rejection, and bitterness.

Punishment is the outcome of disobedience to God's commandments as pronounced in Deuteronomy 28. It gives the Devil and his cohorts the legal grounds to invade lives and afflict those who practise the seeds of the kingdom of darkness, as listed in Galatians 5. The devil has never repented of what he did in the garden of Eden.

The Israelites were the chosen race; they were led out of captivity in Egypt by the powerful hand of God, having served the Egyptians for 430 years. God, through Moses, performed several miracles and led them across the Red Sea on dry land. They witnessed the military might of Pharaoh drown in the same sea they had been miraculously led through. Joy and happiness filled their hearts, and they worshipped the Lord with praises.

During their time in the wilderness, God rained manna and quail for their food (Exod. 16:). He brought forth water from the rock to quench the thirst of the Israel, and turned the bitter waters in Marah and Elim to sweetness (Exod. 17:1–7). God defeated the Amalekites when they came to attack them (Exod. 17:8f).

Yet, when God led Moses to Mount Sinai to receive the set of rules sealed with the blood of covenant for his people, the Israelites took to idol worship, fornication, and adultery. The wrath of God came upon them and they died in thousands Exod. 32). Wickedness and disobedience continued, and God gave up the idea of going with the Israelites because of their hardheartedness. The journey meant to last forty days eventually lasted forty years.

This is the kind of punishment awaiting anyone who disobeys God. With or without God's promises, you become a prey for the Devil once you begin to disobey God. The Devil has no other ministry than to steal, destroy, and kill (John 10:10).

The sons of the prophet Eli erred against the people of Israel and against the commandments of God. The Bible says they were wicked men, abusing the offerings meant for the Lord on the altar and defiling women around town. Thus, God's wrath came upon the household of Eli to reverse their promised priesthood. 'Therefore, the Lord, the God of Israel declares; I promised that your house and your father's house would minister before me forever. But now the Lord declares, far be it from me! Those who honour me I will honour but those who despise me will be disdained' (1 Sam. 2:30).

King Saul disobeyed God, doing what he desired contrary to God's commandments, and his kingdom was taken from him and given to someone else (1 Sam. 15:28).

King David committed adultery with Bathsheba, the wife of Uriah, and eventually killed Uriah to take Bathsheba as his wife. Consequently, God raised His judgement against the household of David. Then the Devil took over and afflicted David's household with violence.

King Solomon also disobeyed God's commandment and broke his covenant with God by marrying foreign wives and bringing idolatry into Israel. Then God pronounced his punishment and declared that the once united, glorious, and golden nation of Israel would be divided into two during the reign of Solomon's son.

After the nation of Israel was divided into two according to God's judgement, God caused enemies from neighbouring countries to invade Jerusalem and Judah. They took away the children of Israel to Babylon as slaves. They served in the empires of the Babylonians, Medians, Persians, Greeks, and Romans until the birth of our Lord Jesus Christ.

You need to ask yourself this question constantly: 'Am I going through a trial, persecution, punishment, or affliction?'

The Devil always attacks when he senses that you are a bearer of God's glory and blessings. All he wants to do is to steal, destroy, and kill destinies as he did to Adam and Eve in the garden of Eden.

Jesus has come to give abundant life. and the Word of God has settled our victory (Rev. 12:10–11). The Devil is not prepared to spare anyone, particularly believers, but there is an assurance of victory for all believers provided by the outpouring of the blood of the Lamb on the cross at Calvary. Jesus was hung on the tree of anguish to nail your infirmities with Him on the cross. He conquered the Devil to give you and I an irrevocable victory (Isa. 53:4–6).

Let's consider a fundamental truth about God's ordinances for man and creatures in the history of creation. The Bible says, 'God blessed them and said to them, "Be fruitful and increase in number, fill the earth and subdue it, rule over the fish of the sea, and the birds of the air, and over every living creature that moves on the ground"' (Gen. 1:28).

Has it ever occurred to you that it is an abomination for you to use any creatures as a source of empowerment or protection for yourself? Many people have done this and still doing so. You are meant to rule over them; they are meant to serve as your food

(Gen. 1:26). Anything contrary is a desecration of the temple of God within you. God formed you to be empowered with the Holy Spirit to do exploits on earth like Himself.

Let me be emphatic. From the day of humanity's expulsion from the garden of Eden, we lost the physical presence of God. We regained it by the experience of the Holy Spirit's baptism by fire at Pentecost.

God is not going to come down to the level of man; He has set a platform for man to come to His level. If you use the powers that come from creatures, then you are contaminating the temple of God within you. You are asking the Holy Spirit to vacate your life, thereby impeding the fulfilment of God's promises.

Surely, God will not honour His promises to people who worship animal idols. Instead, they are doomed to eternal damnation. 'But the cowardly, the unbelieving, the vile, the murderers, the sexually immoral, those who practice magic arts "witchcraft", the idolatry and all liars, their place will be in the fiery lake of burning sulphur, this is the second death' (Rev. 21:8).

The only channel that can lead you to safe arrival at the Promised Land is to worship God in Spirit and truth. 'Yet a time is coming and has now come when the true worshippers will worship the Father in Spirit and truth, for they are the kind of worshippers the Father seeks' (John 4:23).

All the powers and principalities, including the wicked spirits in the high places, operate with the use of vegetation and beasts to destroy their victims. They plant the images to attack and manipulate you in your dreams. All the agents of the Devil, such as witch doctors, voodoo masters, and the prophets of Baal, also use these objects.

Each time you consult with them for solutions to your problems, they insert their contact points – otherwise known as monitoring gadgets – through incisions, and give you concoctions that manipulate your life in the future through afflictions and bigger problems than the ones that led you to them in the first instance.

These are their operational procedures: they diagnose your problems with the power of divination or whatever medium they may be using, then prescribe parts of birds, snakes, and other animals, or leaves and roots. They prepare concoctions for you to drink, or burn them to powder to be applied via incisions in your body. These become contact points for the invasion of your spirit. They monitor and manipulate your life from the spiritual realm.

Your blood is extracted to serve as a covenant that you are handing yourself over to them. You personally relinquish your spiritual well-being to take the mark of the beast upon your life. The mark of the beast is applied as an incision.

The Bible says:

A third angel followed them and said in a loud voice. If anyone worships the beast and his image and receives his mark on the forehead or on the hand, he too will drink of the wine of God's fury, which has been poured full strength into the cup of his wrath. He will be tormented with burning sulphur in the presence of the holy angels and of the Lamb. And the smokes of their torment rises for ever and ever. There is no rest day or night for those who worship the beast and his image or for any one who receives the mark of his name. (Rev. 14:9–11)

Beloved, don't get frightened. These practices are real, but your deliverance is also real. It is guaranteed with the blood of our Lord Jesus Christ. Rejoice. Your Redeemer lives forever.

The Holy Spirit is the only source of empowerment for believers. He is the only communication Agent to maintaining sweet fellowship with God for speedy fulfilment of promises. The Bible says, 'When Abram was ninety nine years old, the Lord appeared to him and said, I am God Almighty; walk before me and be blameless. I will confirm my covenant between me and you and will greatly increase your numbers' (Gen. 17:1–2).

It is impossible to please God without holiness. Holiness is the act of obedience to the commandment of God. He doesn't need your assistance to do what He wants to do. He wants you to walk before Him and be holy to witness the accelerated fulfilment of His promises.

When Jesus entered the temple in Jerusalem, He took the scroll to read from the book of Isaiah:

The Spirit of the Sovereign Lord is upon me, because the Lord has anointed me to preach good news to the poor, He has sent me to bind up the broken-hearted, to proclaim freedom for the captives and release from darkness for the prisoners, to proclaim the year of the Lord's favour and the day of vengeance of our God to comfort all who mourn, and provide for those who grieve in Zion—to bestow on them a crown of beauty instead of ashes, the oil of gladness instead of mourning and a garment of praise instead of a spirit of despair. They will be called oaks of righteousness, a planting of the Lord for the display of his splendour. (Isa. 61:1–3).

Without the Holy Spirit, man is a failure. The above Bible text found fulfilment in the person of our Lord Jesus Christ. He read it to proclaim His manifesto and did exactly as His Father in heaven sent Him.

Idolatry is a major barrier to the fulfilment of the promises of God. Most of our cultural and traditional practices including some religious doctrines that are rooted in idol worshipping. Idolatry provokes the wrath of God upon any individual, family, community, church, or nation that practises it. It makes God jealous and turns His anger into a consuming fire.

When you worship idols, nature will react violently against you to enforce curses relating to the sin you have committed (Deut. 28:15–65). Your loved ones will turn against you; your spouse will become negative to you at home and ultimately divorce you. Hatred, rejection, and disappointment will become the repeated experience in place of favour. Children will turn against their parents. Idolatry gives birth to generational poverty, sickness, setbacks, stagnancy, limitation, and every negative tendency.

Egypt and Ethiopia were once powerful nations in the early history of the world. Civilisation began in Egypt. Other nations of the world trooped to Egypt for economic, political, cultural, and educational empowerment.

But Egyptians took to idol worshipping. They planted shrines for idols virtually in every corner of Egypt and relegated God to the background. Then the anger of God arose against Egypt and Ethiopia. Isaiah, the son of Amoz, was sent to walk around Egypt naked and barefooted for three years to warn the Egyptians to repent from their idolatrous practices, else God would send enemies to invade (Isa. 19:1–10; 20:1-6).

The consequences of idolatry are terrible and devastating. It brings ruin to a whole generation and revokes God's blessings. I urge you to reflect on your foundation and where you came from. Consider the numbers of idol altars that were built by your ancestors, including parents and grandparents. These need to be destroyed by you as born-again children of God. Consider the cultural and traditional practices you are still supporting that give credence to idol worshipping. You too could be the Gideon of your generation.

The Bible says that the Israelites took to idol worshipping and God handed them over to the Midianites for punishment. The Midianites came aggressively against the Israelites. They ruined all the Israelites' crops and livestock and tents. They did not spare anything all the way to Gaza. The Bible says that they invaded like swarms of locusts, ravaged the land of Israel, and impoverished them until they cried to the Lord for help (Judg. 6:1–6).

This is an example of how God will hand over anyone who turns away from God to practice idolatry. There is need for you to personally renounce and destroy every altar built to worship idols in your generation. Silence all the demons on assignment against your destiny, who often lead to repeated negative history in your family.

The Bible says that when the Israelites cried to God for help, God sent his prophet to deliver His message. God assigned

Gideon to destroy the altar of Baal built by his father and raise another altar for God. This may be your next assignment; you may be the Gideon of this generation.

The Promised Gift of the Messiah

The manifestation of the Son of God on earth was the most incredible miracle ever to happen in the history of God's intervention in the affairs of humankind. It is the manifestation of God's faithfulness to His promise of redemption and restoration through the offspring of the woman; a promise that culminated in the birth of our Lord Jesus Christ by the Virgin Mary.

The judgement raised against Satan, the serpent, over his deceit of the first couple caused them to disobey God's commandment. It was packaged to favour man. It contained the ministry of the Saviour, with the mandate to execute the final defeat of the serpent, thus setting man free from whatever bondage the sin of disobedience had plunged mankind into. The judgement set a standard against the devil and his kingdom. 'And I will put enmity between you and the woman and between your offspring and hers; he will crush your head and you will strike his feet' (Gen. 3:15).

The ministry of our Lord Jesus Christ finds its roots in this promise and marks the beginning of the gospel. The offspring of the woman is Jesus; the bruising of the heel is the crucifixion of our Lord Jesus Christ on the cross at Calvary; the crushing of the serpent's head is Christ's victory over the Devil (Heb. 2:14). The ultimate victory will be the final appearance of Christ (Rev. 20:10).

The promise of Messiah was also contained in the covenant promise of blessing for Abraham, that through his offspring, the nations of the world would be blessed. The promise in this passage also found fulfilment in the text of John 3:16: 'For God so loved the world and gave His only begotten son that whosoever believed in Him will not die but have an everlasting life.' This messianic promise was included in the covenant promise with Isaac and Jacob as an everlasting covenant, and was ultimately confirmed to David (2 Kings 7:12-17).

The Great Deliverance

The deliverance of the Israelites out of Egypt by Moses symbolised the final deliverance of humanity from the hands of the Devil by the Messiah. The deliverance and the journey through the wilderness were manifestations of miracles, signs, and wonders enabled by the covenant promise of God.

God used Moses to perform many miracles in Egypt, including the ten plagues, the miracle of dividing the Red Sea for the Israelites to walk through on dry land, and the miracles of manna and quail from heaven and waters from the rock to quench the thirst of the Israelites in the wilderness. Later miracles, including dividing the river Jordan and the fall of the wall of Jericho to usher the Israelites into the Promised Land, were part of God's faithfulness in fulfilling the promises He made to Abraham to 'make you a great nation'. God established a nation of royal priesthood, a holy nation of the people of God, named Israel.

When the nation of Israel was established, God was the President. He ruled the nation directly from heaven (theocracy) and raised prophets to reveal His plan of salvation through the promised Messiah (2 Kings 7:12-17).

Isaiah's Prophecy about Jesus

Isaiah lived in Judah in the eighth century BC, during the days of Assyrian insurgence. Isaiah prophesised to King Ahaz in Jerusalem in 735–715 BC, and to King Hezekiah in Judah in 715–686 BC. He spoke clearly about the political situation of their time. His message to both kings was that no human power could stand in the way of Assyria. Thus, Judah was not to rely on or form any alliance with Egypt or other nations, but to rely only on God's power to protect Zion and God's chosen people.

Three hundred years before the prophet Isaiah began his ministry, King David had drawn the struggling tribe of Israel together and subdued their enemies and neighbouring groups to carve out a secured state. This became known as the golden age of Israel. Evil forces crept into the state of Israel and caused the golden age to lose its lustre when Solomon ascended the throne.

Solomon created great discontent by his luxurious living, influenced by idol worshipping and oppressive ways. Following the death of King Solomon, the division of the once united kingdom of Israel began. Military struggle, false worship, weak leadership, internal confusion, and external aggression characterised the lives of the two nations, Israel and Judah, down to the eighth century BC.

In the first half of the eighth century BC, Israel and Judah attained a strength in prosperity and security they had not witnessed before. They were freed from the danger of being destroyed by other powers and were ruled by capable kings: Jeroboam II (793–753 BC) in the northern kingdom of Israel, and Uzziah (792–740 BC) in the southern kingdom of Judah.

Regrettably, the last half of eighth century BC was a different story. Assyria began a policy of expansion and conquest, which brought the destruction of Israel and left Judah under the condition of paying tribute. It was in the year the good king Uzziah died that God called Isaiah. Isaiah was commissioned to function as a major prophet, to reveal the pattern and process of the coming Messiah.

During Isaiah's encounter with God in a temple worship experience, Isaiah reacted as he should. **"woe unto me" I cried, I am ruined! For I am a man of unclean lips and I live among a people of unclean lips and my eyes have seen the King, the Lord Almighty (Isa. 6:5).** During a visitation by God, guilt must become the recognition of our personal sinful nature and its devastating consequences. Genuine penitence occurs when a sinner consciously stands before his Creator and sees the contrast between his sinful nature and a pure, holy God. This wonderful experience often occurs during worship. Worship helps us to hear God and understand Him as One who meets us at our sinful level to offer grace and call us to His marvellous grace and service.

After the prophet had sought and found cleansing from God, he was set for glorious and noble service, to predict the exact details of the coming Messiah.

Beloved, atonement cleanses and makes us ready for God's service. Isaiah's holy encounter with God in the temple was a grace beyond description for glorious call to service. 'Then one of the seraphs flew to me with a live coal in his hand, which he had taken with tongs from the altar. With it, he touched my mouth and said, "see this has touched your lips, your guilt is taken away and your sin atoned for"' (Isa. 6:6–7).

Isaiah's positive response to his call to service is a motivation to others for the work of the ministry. Although the call came distinctly to the prophet Isaiah, in principle the same call comes to all of us. Our obedient response must always be, 'Here am I, send me', so that multitudes may come to salvation.

The Seraphs and the Power of Worship

The Seraphs are the burning ones: angelic members of the heavenly court of the Most High God. Their main responsibility is to worship. They worship God ceaselessly, day and night. They cover their faces in the presence of God and carry out His directives. However, they are not messengers to God's people like other angels.

Isaiah saw God's glory and became convinced that prestige and honour should be ascribed only to almighty God, the King of Kings and the Lord of Lords, God of the universe. The Bible says, 'At the sound of their (Seraphs) voices the doorpost and the thresholds shook and the temple was filled with smoke' (Isa. 6:4).

God is morally pure and distinct in holiness, so we are to fall in worship of Him and confess our sin. Isaiah encountered God in the temple and reacted as he should. He was aware of the difference between the holy Creator and the unholy creatures, as well as the consequences of seeing God face-to-face. Such a wonderful encounter provided the opportunity for Isaiah to discover his sinful nature, forgiveness of sin, and a calling to serve in the glorious mission.

As humans, we need to meet God on the platform of 'sinful me' and 'pure God' for a positive divine transformation to be made in us, and for us to be made fit to serve in the glorious offices of God (Eph. 4:11).

Penitence is total spiritual breakdown preceding remoulding for the works of the kingdom of God. It is the manifestation of the seventh spirit of God (Isa. 11:2). The fear of God must be activated first, then a broken and contrite heart manifested on the outside, to bring about humility, confession, and submissiveness.

This is how it came on King David when he committed heinous sin and he wrote Psalm 51.

> The tongue is one of the most powerful forces on earth. It contains life and death. Learn how to use it.

A seraph atoned for the sins of Isaiah with a live coal touched on his tongue. The fire of the Holy Spirit atoned for his sins and made him ready for God's work. You and I need such divine encounters to become more effective in the work of His kingdom.

'Then I heard the voice of the Lord saying, "whom shall I send and who shall go for us? Then I said "here am I, send me"' (v8). Having being purged of his sins and made clean with the fire of the Holy Spirit, Isaiah was now qualified to serve as a member of God's council on earth, mandated with bringing God's promises into fulfilment. Isaiah responded with obedience: 'Here am I, send me.' (Isaiah 6:8)

The call came distinctly to the prophet. The same call comes to many of God's people. How do we answer His call? God is still crying, 'Who shall I send? Who shall go for us to perform specific assignments that will facilitate the fulfilment of covenant promises?' My prayer for you and I as you read this book is that you will see the Lord, hear His call, and respond obediently, in Jesus's name. 'He said, "Go and tell this people: Be ever hearing but never understanding, be ever seeing but never perceiving. Make the hearts of these people calloused; make their ears dull and close their eyes. Otherwise, they might see with their eyes, hear with their ears, understand with their hearts, and turn and be blessed"' (Isa. 6:9–10).

This is the mystery about the revelation of the Messiah to mankind, particularly among the Jewish people. Jesus's appearance never gave any indication to those around him that He was their promised Messiah. Those who lacked faith, wisdom, and knowledge of God did not comprehend his parables. His mighty works were intentionally rejected by those who should have known better. Their hearts were hardened. His own expected a political myth or a military marshal, but He came lowly, as the Lamb of God to be slaughtered. His birth did not suggest that a Messiah had been born. The authorities who got a hint of his birth sought to kill him. This was the deliberate plan of God to fulfil His promises.

Ministers of God must not allow opposition to the truth of the gospel by unbelievers to be the reason for their failures. What was true for the Master is also true for the servant. 'He came to that which was his own but his own did not receive him. Yet to all who received him, to those who believed in his name, he gave the right to become children of God' (John 1:11–12).

God used Isaiah for a systematic revelation of the coming Messiah in a way that was incomprehensible to man. Isaiah's prophecies were referred to in the New Testament far more often than all the other prophets in the Bible put together. The revelation of the coming Messiah came as a sign from God: 'Therefore, the Lord Himself will give you a sign. The virgin will be with a child and will give birth to a son and will call him Immanuel' (Isa. 7:14). Here, God employed the most complete sign of communication ever: the birth of a son by a virgin, whose very name reveals God's intentions to be with man and to be the God of his children. Immanuel means 'God with us'.

When the kingdom of Judah was threatened by a confederation of enemies from the north, King Ahaz was terrified. God sent Isaiah to calm down the king with assurance that the evil forces would not prevail. King Ahaz was also encouraged to 'ask for a sign', but the stubborn king refused.

God directed Isaiah's prophecy according to his covenant promise to David (2 Sam. 7:13). He promised a much greater sign: namely, that the virgin would conceive and bear a son. The period that it would take for the Immanuel-child to reach the age of accountability was used as a chronological measurement. Before that time span expired, Judah's current threat would dissipate, which in reality happened. More important, however, was the fact that a much greater deliverance was needed in Israel. It would be provided by the actual arrival of Immanuel, who is Jesus Christ.

The immediate context suggests a miracle. The king had been challenged to ask for a sign, either 'in the depth, or in the height above' (11). This indicates something phenomenal. Ahaz refused the proffered sign, claiming that such would 'tempt' Jehovah (again implying the supernatural).

Forever, the Word of God is settled. A virgin, Eve, was deceived by Satan to enable his attack on humanity, causing the fall of man in the garden of Eden. But the love of God, expressed by His infallible Word, brought salvation to mankind.

Transfiguratively, another virgin, Mary, was raised to conceive and give birth to the promised Messiah, the Son of God, who eventually conquered Satan on the cross at Calvary and set humanity free from the bondage of sin, according to His Word spoken over four thousand years before: 'And I will put an enmity between you and the woman and between your offspring and hers, he will crush your head and you will strike his heel' (Gen. 3:15). The promised birth of our Lord Jesus Christ, Immanuel, was a blessing to the entire world. The first Adam brought sin and suffering to the world; the second Adam, Jesus, brought truth, grace, and salvation to the world.

Isaiah prophesied thus: 'For to us a child is born, to us a son is given, and the government will be on his shoulders. And he will be called Wonderful Counsellor, Mighty God, Everlasting Father, Prince of peace. Of the increase of his government and peace there will be no end He will reign on David's throne and over his kingdom, establishing and upholding it with justice and righteousness from that time on and forever. The seal of the Lord Almighty will accomplish this' (Isa. 9:6–7). This was written between 701 and 681 BC, about seven hundred years before the birth of Jesus.

Isaiah speaks of a son who will be called 'Mighty God' and 'Eternal Father', and also indicates that this son will reign on the throne of King David, and His reign will be everlasting. The Bible says, 'When your days are over and you rest with your fathers, I will raise up your offspring to succeed you, who will come from your own body, and I will establish his kingdom. He is the one who will build a house for my Name. and I will establish the throne of his kingdom forever' (2 Sam. 7:12–13).

King David was the great, God-obeying king. God promised King David that the reign from David's throne would be everlasting. This promise was fulfilled in Jesus Christ, who is a descendant of King David, and whose reign is indeed everlasting.

Today, the teachings of Jesus Christ preside over the lives of as many as 2 billion Christians and 1.5 billion Muslims worldwide. The New Testament says that Jesus will return in the future, and His kingdom will have no end:

And from Jesus Christ, who is the faithful witness, the firstborn from the dead, and the ruler of the kings of the earth. To him who loves us and has freed us from our sins by his blood, and has made us to be a kingdom and priests to serve his God and Father, to him be glory and power forever and ever! Amen. Look, he is coming with the clouds and every eye will see him, even those who pierced him, and all the peoples of the earth will mourn because of him; so shall it be. Amen. (Rev. 1:5–7)

Israel's faith was based on their historical experience; people trusted God because the Israelites had experienced God's mighty acts in history. Israel developed its faith in God because God had acted in the past, and they anticipated He would continue to act in the future according to His promises.

One promise was centred on the coming Messiah, whom God would send to deliver the Israelites from political and other forms of slavery. The Messiah would be a unique bearer of the Spirit of God, giving believers the power to do works of justice and judgement.

Isaiah accurately predicted the genealogy of the coming Messiah. Upon the Messiah, the Spirit of God would manifest seven attributes: 'A shoot will come up from the stump of Jesse, from his roots a branch will bear fruit. The Spirit of the Lord will rest on him, the Spirit of wisdom and of understanding, the Spirit of Counsel and of power, the Spirit of knowledge and of the fear of the Lord' (Isaiah 11:1–2).

The Seven Characteristics and Attributes of the Holy Spirit
1. The Spirit of the Lord
2. The Spirit of Wisdom
3. The Spirit of Understanding
4. The Spirit of Counsel
5. The Spirit of Might
6. The Spirit of Knowledge
7. The Spirit of Fear of the Lord.

The Spirit of Lord
The first of the seven Spirits mentioned by the prophet Isaiah is the Spirit of the Lord. This is also known as the Spirit of

Lordship or Spirit of Dominion. He is the One who comes upon the anointed to give boldness and the sense of dominion. He puts the anointed in charge of situations.

The Spirit of Wisdom
The Spirit of Wisdom is often defined as the ability to apply knowledge, but that is not entirely correct when you are talking about wisdom in the context of Holy Spirit. The Spirit of Wisdom is the One who brings you the wisdom of God. Wisdom is a force; it is divine insight into the plan and purpose of God; it is the understanding of spiritual things. Wisdom can also be defined as the insight of knowledge, the controlling power of insight, insight into reality (truth), and foresight.

The Spirit of Understanding
The apostle Paul prayed for the Ephesians, saying, 'May the eyes of your understanding being enlightened' (1:18). He also prayed that they might be able to understand with all saints what is the breadth, length, depth, and height of love, and to know the love of Christ, which passes knowledge (3:18–19). The Spirit of Understanding is the ability to understand the things of God.

The Spirit of Counsel
The Spirit of Counsel is the fourth of the seven spirits of God as listed by Isaiah. It is the One who guides your inner being and orders your steps. The psalmist put it this way: 'I will bless the Lord, who hath given me counsel, my reins also instruct me in the night seasons' (Ps. 16:7).

David referred to the Spirit of Counsel as his inward man, who instructs him in the night seasons. This Spirit tells us what to do and what not to do, and directs us in all our affairs. The Spirit of Counsel gently whispers to our minds to change our direction when we are heading towards danger.

The Spirit of Counsel is our miracle producer. He directs our thoughts and footsteps to do things and to succeed where others fail. He is our personal guiding angel who instructs our minds silently on what to do when all hope is lost. He is supernatural; He cannot be confused. He knows the way out of every crisis in our lives. He knows the solution to all our problems. His full name is Wonderful Counsellor, directing our path lest we dash our feet on stones. He leads us to the zone full of favour, just like Isaac, the son of Abraham (Gen. 26:3–4).

The Spirit of Counsel is also called an extraordinary strategist. One of His extraordinary strategies can be found in the rescue of Israelites from the hands of Pharaoh (Exod. 14:15–16).

The Spirit of Might

The Spirit of Might is the fifth of the seven spirits of God. There was a man in the Old Testament who was a judge operating in the Spirit of Might. His name was Samson.

Samson did not have the Spirit of Wisdom like Moses and Joshua; otherwise, he would not have done some of the dumb things he did. However he had the Spirit of Might (Judges 14:5–6). When the Spirit of Might rests upon your life, He causes you to be bold and empowered, to act with supernatural strength unsought for and overcome every obstacle in your life.

When Samuel anointed David, the Bible says the Holy Spirit rested upon him. David went back to the field to take care of the flock, and lo and behold, there came a lion wanting to devour a lamb. David, being filled with the Spirit of Might, charged after the lion, killed it, and delivered the lamb.

On another occasion, it was a bear who came, and David dealt with it in the same way. When David eventually stood against Goliath, the Spirit of Might on him reduced Goliath to a beast like the lion and the bear. These magnificent acts of gallantry were not performed by David's own strength, but by the anointing of the Spirit of Might that was upon him.

The Spirit of Might is the supernatural, dynamic ability to make changes. I pray that as you read this book, you will be anointed with the Spirit of Might in Jesus's name. Amen.

The Spirit of Knowledge
The Spirit of Knowledge is the sixth spirit of God. The difference between successful, victorious Christians and the ones who are not successful does not depend much on their talents but on the knowledge they have. Your limitations or achievements today are a direct function and reflection of your knowledge.

Knowledge is acquaintance – that is, being aware of something. It is different from intellectual knowledge. Knowledge from the Holy Spirit is imparted into your human spirit. It transcends the mental realm (1 Cor. 2:12). We have not received this world's spirit; instead, we have received the Spirit sent by God, so that we may know all that God has given us.

This revelation knowledge transcends scientific knowledge or human discovery.

However, Scripture says, 'What no one ever thought could happen, is the very thing God prepared for those who love him. It was to us that God made known his secrets by means of his Spirit. The Spirit searches everything, even the hidden depths of God's purposes' (1 Cor. 2:9–10).

This is the Spirit of Knowledge at work in us, by God who reveals all things to us. I pray that God will endow you with the Spirit of Knowledge.

The Spirit of the Fear of God
This is the last but not the least of the seven Spirits of God. It is also referred to as the Spirit of Reverence (Ps. 111:4–10). This is the Spirit that worked with the priests in the Old Testament. Samuel was both a priest and a prophet to the children of Israel (1 Sam. 12:18).

When the Spirit of Reverence comes into an environment, things change. He disciplines people and set things in order; He makes everyone humble before God. When Ananias and Sapphira misbehaved, He struck them dead, and great fear came upon the people (Acts 5:1–11).

Any time the anointing of God's Spirit becomes strong, something spectacular happens: fear or holy awe or reverence comes upon the people. That's the Spirit of the Fear of the Lord.

The Spirit of the Fear of the Lord makes you diligent in observing the statutes of God all the time. He stops you from sinning against His commandments. Beware: one may be working in the manifestation of the gifts of the Spirit but lacking the Spirit of the Fear of the Lord. This was what happened to the Corinthian church.

The Corinthians were scrambling for Holy Communion (1 Cor. 11:20–22), yet committing abominable sins (1 Cor. 5:1). There was so much envy, strife and division among them that they had no reverence for spiritual things (1 Cor. 3:3–4).

The Spirit of the Fear of God produces humility in a person; He makes you say the truth at all times for fear of God's wrath, and He makes you obey God's authority (commandments).

Paul advises us to '[submit] yourselves one to another in the fear of God' (CITATION). Peter counselled, 'All of you be subject one to another and be clothed with humility, for God resisteth the proud and giveth grace to the humble. Humble yourself therefore under the mighty hand of God that He may exalt you in due time. Yield yourselves therefore to the Holy Spirit, He will cause you to walk in reverence and humility and He will exalt you in due course of time' (1 Pet. 5:5-6).

Clarifying Isaiah 11:10–12

God made the famous prediction in Isaiah 66:8 that a nation would be born in a single day, even before the birth pains come. It is similar to the prophecy of the valley of the dry bones in Ezekiel 37:1–14. These prophecies were fulfilled in May 1948, when Israel declared independence without a war, but then was engulfed in a war with the surrounding nations within hours.

Today, we can see with our own eyes that many of Isaiah's prophecies have found fulfilment with the worldwide dispersion of Jews, the worldwide persecution of Jews, the recent worldwide migration of Jews back to Israel, the recent re-establishment and restoration of Israel, and the worldwide impact that Jews have had.

Beloved, the Word and covenant promises of God stand sure, irrevocable and dependable.

The Birth of Jesus Christ

Many biblical scholars and religious sects have argued that December 25 was not the actual birth date of Jesus Christ. It was just adopted as a day to celebrate the Christian substitute for the Roman festival Saturnalia. Saturnalia was celebrated as the Feast of Sun in the third century, and was actually considered the birth date of the sun god. Roman Catholic priests held a special Mass that day for Christ, and thus it came to be known as 'Christ Mass' or Christmas. Along with the date, several other pagan traditions, rituals, and customs became associated with Christmas, such as decorating fir trees and burning Yule logs.

In my own opinion, that is a great transformation and doesn't pose any serious concern. Our focus must be on this:

For unto us a child is born, unto us a son is given and the government shall be upon his shoulder and his name shall be called Wonderful Counsellor, The Mighty God, The Everlasting Father, The Prince of Peace. Of the increase of his government and peace there shall be no end upon the throne of David and upon his kingdom, to order it, and to establish it with judgement and with justice from henceforth even for ever. The zeal of the Lord of hosts will perform this. (Isa. 9:6–7)

What grace can compare to this? The gift and the transformation this wonderful gift has brought to the world, coupled with the fulfilment of God's promised 'offspring of the woman' in Genesis 3:15, are enough cause for celebration.

And so it was, that, while they were there [in Bethlehem], the days were accomplished that she should be delivered. And she brought forth her firstborn son, and wrapped him in swaddling clothes, and laid him in a manger; because there was no room for them in the inn. (Luke 2:6-7)

While Jesus was the 'only begotten son' of God, Mary had other children too. Jesus was her 'firstborn'. Jesus was born in the manger not because Mary and Joseph were poor, but because there was 'no room in the inn', as there were lots of people who had come to be registered.

The Ministry of Christ

The purpose of Jesus on earth is first and foremost to fulfil all prophecy concerning God's salvation for humanity. That is the will of God the Father, who sent Him. Jesus said of His purpose:

I came that they may have life, and have it abundantly. (John 10:10)

I desire mercy, not sacrifice. For I have not come to call the righteous, but sinners, to repentance. (Matt. 9:13)

He came to give his life as a ransom for many. (Mark 10:45)

He was sent to preach the good news of the Kingdom of God. (Luke 4:43)

He came so that those who believed in him would have eternal life. (John 3:16)

When the time finally came for Jesus to proclaim the gospel of the kingdom of God and set his public ministry in motion, he began by reading from the book of Isaiah:

The Spirit of the Sovereign Lord is on me because the Lord has anointed me to preach good news to the poor; He has sent me to bind up the broken hearted, to proclaim freedom for the captives and release from darkness for the prisoners; to proclaim the year of the Lord's favour and the day of vengeance of our God; to comfort all who mourn, and provide for those who grieve for Zion—to bestow on them a crown of beauty instead of ashes, the oil of gladness instead of mourning and a garment of praise instead of a spirit of despair. They will be called oaks of righteousness, a planting of the Lord for the display of His splendour. (Isa. 61:1–3)

Let us analyse the mandate and the ministry of our Lord Jesus Christ as prophesied by Isaiah and proclaimed by Jesus Himself at the temple in Jerusalem. He systematically implemented the mandate during His three years of ministry, and at His crucifixion on the cross of Calvary, He declared, 'It is finished.'

Jesus's mandate included these things:
- To preach the good news to the poor
- To bind up the broken-hearted
- To proclaim freedom for the captives
- To release prisoners from darkness

- To proclaim the year of the Lord's favour
- To declare the day of vengeance of our Lord
- To comfort all who mourn
- To provide for those who grieve in Zion
- To bestow on them a crown of beauty instead of ashes
- Oil of gladness instead of mourning
- And garment of praise instead of a spirit of despair
- That they may be called oaks of righteousness

How wonderful, and what a huge responsibility: a marvellous mandate from God through His Son to humanity. No wonder He declared that the Son of Man had come to destroy the works of darkness. All these mandates are meant to reverse what the Devil has done to man from the day he caused man to disobey his Creator.

The Spirit of the Lord is on me
Without the Holy Spirit of God, it would be impossible to fulfil the things of God. So Jesus made it clear that His mandate could only be accomplished with the Spirit of God, not by the power or knowledge of man. The Spirit of God, breathed on man at creation, enabled man to keep the perfect relationship with God and excel in all his endeavours. Only the Spirit of God makes ministering for God possible.

To preach the good news to the poor
From the fall of man in the garden of Eden to the birth of Jesus Christ on earth, the inclination of the hearts of men were evil. There was no good news anywhere except hope for the coming of the Messiah. No one could say specifically the form and shape of His messiahship except as found in the revelations of the prophets.

From the dispensational age of conscience through to the dispensation of law, the news was about suffering and hope for the promised Messiah. The birth and ministry of our Lord Jesus Christ brought blessed assurance of life for humanity. John put it this way: 'For the Law was given through Moses, Grace and Truth came through Jesus' (John 1:17).

Jesus's mandate was to bring forgiveness, news of salvation, and eternal life through His death on the cross of Calvary and the power of His resurrection. These He brought to those who are perpetually bound by the power of sin, taking them into the marvellous light and grace of God. Ye shall know the truth and the truth will set you free (John 8:32): only the truth of the gospel gives freedom to the captives.

The word *poor* can be misleading. It does not refer to those who are poor in money, but rather those who are 'poor in spirit'. Other translations for the word *poor* are 'meek', 'humble', or 'afflicted'. This reminds me of Jesus's Sermon on the Mount (Matt. 5:3–5). It is quite straightforward for those who understand human nature. To be poor in spirit is to be spiritually low.

A poor, meek, or humble person in the Spirit will be diligent and willing to listen to the gospel. A proud and arrogant person will always think that he has everything and may not be interested in hearing about the gospel. However, this does not mean that Jesus only came to preach the good news to humble persons. Not at all. He also preached to the proud and the arrogant, but it was a futile exercise since they refused to listen.

To bind up the broken-hearted

Jesus came to be a healer of souls (Isa. 53:5). The term 'bind up' is an expression used to describe emotional, psychological, and spiritual healing, and this is part of God's programme of salvation (Ps. 147:3).

What does it mean to be broken-hearted? This describes people who are ill in the soul and spiritually depressed by the circumstances of the world. Those who have experienced disappointment have not found fulfilment. They have been hurt by people's cruelties or the affliction of the Devil and his cohorts.

Jews in exile, thinking of their decimated homeland and destroyed capital city, would know exactly what it meant to be broken-hearted. The idea that Jesus is a soul healer reminds me of the story of how Jesus called Matthew, the tax collector, to be one of his disciples (Matt. 9:9–13). As a tax collector, Matthew would have been hated by the majority of his own people. By accepting him and forgiving him, Jesus healed his broken heart and gave him purpose and dignity.

To proclaim freedom for the captives **and** *to release prisoners from darkness*

The core mission of our Lord Jesus was to bring freedom and sight to those who are spiritually bound and spiritually blind. What bounds and blinds man spiritually is sin, and death is the wages for sin. Jesus's mandate was to forgive us our sins, thereby releasing sinners from bondage and from darkness into His marvellous light.

To proclaim the year of the Lord's favour

This can be translated as 'the acceptable year of the Lord'. It also corresponds with the 'day of salvation' in Isaiah 49:8, and the 'year of my redemption' in Isaiah 63:4. We should not take 'year' as a literal year, but rather a length of time with definite limits. The Lord's favour, therefore, will not last forever. There is a window in time during which people can repent and turn to the Lord. We know this year ends with Jesus's second coming.

To declare the day of vengeance of our Lord

Notice here that the Lord provides a 'year' for His favour, but only spends a 'day' on vengeance. Also, the vengeance comes after the year of His favour. This gives us an idea of how God has been long-suffering and patient throughout the Old Testament.

It begins with the people of Noah's time. He tells Noah to build an ark, which takes years. We know from what we read in 2 Peter that Noah preached righteousness to his generation. Noah's contemporaries could have repented, but chose not to. We also learned how God called out Abraham and established a covenant of blessing and salvation with him and his descendants.

This included the Davidic covenant up to the birth and death of our Lord Jesus Christ. These are the years of the Lord's favour. Jesus compares His second coming to the flood in Noah's day (Matt. 24:36–44). Revelation 1:7 gives us a picture of what Jesus's second coming will be like.

To comfort all who mourn

That the Lord will bring comfort to those who are mourning and grieving is a common theme in the Bible (Jer. 31:13; Matt. 5:4). A common form of mourning is when a loved one dies.

(Read 1 Thess. 4:13–14.) However, I think that there is another kind of mourning one feels when one knows that one is not right with God because of shortcomings, transgressions, ignorance, and sins. Paul calls this 'godly sorrow' that leads to repentance (2 Cor. 7:8–10).

To provide for those who grieve in Zion

The mandate gives three specific blessings for those who are godly mourners. The first is 'to bestow on them a crown of beauty instead of ashes'. In Jewish culture, it was customary to sprinkle ashes on one's head as a sign of mourning and repentance. We have an example from Ezekiel 27 of people mourning the destruction of the city of Tyre. God says, 'I have seen and accepted your repentance; I will replace your crown of ashes with a crown of great beauty' (2 Tim. 4:8). In the New Testament, we also see this crown called the 'crown of life' and the 'crown of glory'.

The second specific blessing is 'to bestow on them the oil of gladness instead of mourning'. Again, we have to understand the culture. When a Jewish person was in mourning, he or she would not put on any cosmetic lotions or perfumes (2 Sam. 14:2). However, when people were happy or joyful, we see examples of them being anointed with olive oil or perfumes (Pss. 45:7–8; 133:1–2). The 'oil of gladness' could also mean the anointing of the Holy Spirit that accompanies the joy of the Lord coming upon a person. That holy joy replaces the sorrow that comes with a heavy heart.

The third blessing is 'to bestow on them the garment of praise instead of a spirit of despair'. This alludes to how, when one was in mourning, one would dress in sackcloth – an ugly, scratchy, uncomfortable garment. Despair and distress was displayed physically by one's clothes.

The coming dispensation of His kingdom would change all that (Rev. 21:1–6). No longer would you despair; you would be joyful and praising God. I cannot help thinking of how this relates to the beautiful white robes the saints wear in heaven, as described in Revelation 7:9. Palm branches were used on festive occasions as a sign of celebration and praise.

They may be called oaks of righteousness
Again, we see people compared to plants, as we saw in Isaiah 60:21. Notice here that the people are compared to oaks. Oaks are strong, enduring plants, not easily swayed or destroyed, with deep roots. Such people are the display of the Lord's splendour.

The Lamb of God

The story of the Lamb of God began in the Old Testament, when Abraham responded in obedience to God's demands for him to offer his only, covenant-promised son, Isaac, as sacrifice for Him on Mount Moriah (Gen. 22:1–14). While Abraham was preparing to offer Isaac as sacrifice, he faithfully declared to his son that God would provide. His trust and faithful obedience to God manifested in the provision of the Lamb of God.

But the angel of the Lord called out to him from heaven, 'Abraham! Abraham' 'here I am' he replied. Do not lay a hand on the boy he said. Do not do anything to him. Now I know that you fear God, because you have not withheld from me your son, your only son. Abraham looked up and there in a thicket he saw a ram caught by its horns. He went over and took the ram and sacrificed it as a burn offering instead of his son. (Gen. 22:11–13)

Abraham demonstrated an unusual faith and obedience. God responded with a covenant promise of blessing and salvation for humanity, from which Jesus Christ, the Son of God and the Lamb of God, was produced.

Jesus came as the Lamb of God to be sacrificially slaughtered for the propitiation and remission of our sins. He came to remove our guiltiness and suffering in exchange for eternal life (Isa. 53:3–5). He restored the abundant life prepared for us from eternity past by our Father in heaven (John 10:10). John 1 refers to Jesus Christ as the perfect and ultimate sacrifice for sin.

What does this mean to sinful man? It simply means a divine exchange, an atonement for our sin, iniquities, and transgressions. The thorn and thistle which represent human suffering and death, as pronounced by God in Genesis 3, was wrapped as crown and pressed upon the head of Jesus Christ. The Bible says, 'Surely he took up our infirmities and carried our sorrows, yet we considered him stricken by God, smitten by him, and afflicted. But he was pierced for our transgressions, he was crushed for our iniquities; the punishment that brought us peace was upon him and by his wounds we are healed' (Isa. 53:4–5).

An unusual miracle took place when the Lamb of God was offered as a living sacrifice on the cross at Calvary. The Bible says, 'At that moment the curtain of the temple was torn in two from top to bottom. The earth shook and the rocks split. The tombs broke open and the bodies of many holy people who had died were raised to life' (Matt. 27:51–53).

The miracle of that Good Friday caused a cosmic eruption that disturbed the whole creation to release everyone under the captivity of sin and death, including those who were enslaved by the Devil. Jesus declared, 'So if the Son sets you free, you will be free indeed' (John 8:36). It is total freedom from everything that runs contrary to God's blessing in Genesis 1:26–28.

CHAPTER 5

God's Manifold Promises

Rejection

My definition of 'rejection' is the act of refusing to accept or declining to believe a person and his viewpoint. Rejection elicits emotional pain so sharp that it affects our thinking faculties. It erodes our confidence and self-esteem to the point that many give up hope of survival and develop depression. Some have committed suicide, burying their destinies in the grave and thereby giving victory to the Devil.

On the other hand, rejection has advantages and value. It enables a believer to look up to God for divine help to actualize potential, as written by King David in Psalm 121. It enables you to stretch forward and leap beyond your comfortable environment into the world. It also enables you to discover yourself and grow the seeds of talent planted in you by your Maker, so you become a testimony to impact and transform other people's lives.

You can be rejected if you have a trait of leadership in you. You can be rejected if you are an agent of change and truth. You can be rejected by those who are jealous of you. You can also be rejected for your negative attitude.

Let's draw our lesson from others in the Bible – those who have gone through the experience of rejection, yet have excelled amid the storms.

Joseph was rejected by his brothers because of his leadership trait: 'Do you intend to reign over us? Will you actually rule us?' (Gen. 37:8). But Joseph focused on God, and he was exalted far above comprehension of man.

Jesus Christ, though He was the expected Messiah, was rejected by his own people. The Bible says, 'He came to that which was his own, but his own did not receive him' (John 1:11). They preferred Barabbas, the criminal, and rejected Jesus. They demanded that Jesus be crucified and got him killed on the cross at Calvary.

But Jesus rose from the death and ascended to sit with His Father in His glory. The Bible says, 'When my father and my mother forsake me then the Lord will take over' (Ps. 27:10).

Humans were rejected and expelled from the garden of Eden for an act of disobedience against God's commandment. But with grace and mercy, God promised deliverance and restoration (Gen. 3:15).

Forgiveness and Sanctification

'God is not a man that he should lie, neither the son of man that he should repent' (Num. 23:19). Sin is rebellion against God. All persons without exception are under the dominion of sin, starting with our primary ancestors, Adam and Eve.

The origin of sin is Satan. He introduced its long and malicious reign into human history when he beguiled Eve in Genesis 3. Since then, sin has been like a malignant cancer upon the face of human history, distorting and disfiguring the relationship of humanity with God. It is a device for Satan to steal and destroy the blessings of God in the life of humankind.

Satan set the stage for Adam and Eve to disobey the explicit command of God. Every person who has ever lived has followed their example. God's grace has made an escape route for forgiveness through our Lord Jesus Christ, the Lamb of God.

At this stage in the history of humanity, forgiveness and the restoration of man to the original image and likeness of God have become the thrust of God's agenda.

Forgiveness is the nature of God. It is the upper chamber of love and the product of mercy and grace.

Forgiveness is the core mandate in the ministry of our Lord Jesus Christ. It facilitates restoration of man to the original image and likeness of God. Without forgiveness, there can never be blessing and eternal life.

The Bible says:

This is the covenant I will make with the house of Israel, after that time declares the Lord, I will put my laws in their minds and write it in their hearts. I will be their God and they will be my people. No longer will a man teach his neighbour or man his brothers saying, Know the Lord, because they will all know me, from the least of them to the greatest. For I will forgive their wickedness and will remember their sins no more. (Heb. 8:10–12)

The promise of forgiveness is meant for the household of Jacob, the born-again children of God who have genuinely confessed and repented of their sins. This also translates to mean that God will establish Himself in the hearts of His people as the one true God. He will give them new hearts and a new spirit that will forever fear and honour the one sovereign God.

God wants every person to know Him as a loving, heavenly Father through a faithful relationship with His Son, Jesus Christ, the Lamb of God. The Bible says, 'If my people, who are called by my name, will humble themselves and pray and seek my face and turn from their wicked ways, then will I hear from heaven and will forgive their sin and will heal their land' (2 Chron. 7:14).

The above passage lays out conditions that must be met by all believers to receive forgiveness and restoration from the Lord. These include humility, prayer, and seeking the face of the Lord, completely turning away from our wickedness.

God the Father invested Himself in the person of our Lord Jesus Christ. The Bible says, 'For God so loved the world, that he gave his only begotten Son, that whosoever believeth in him should not perish, but have everlasting life' (John 3:16). The most profound expression of God's love for mankind is the gift of His only begotten Son to be our Saviour. This simply translates that God, who is love, gave Himself away as a living sacrifice to His subjects so they could receive forgiveness. The

Bible says, 'But God demonstrates His own love toward us, in that while we were yet sinners, Christ died for us' (Rom. 5:8).

Forgiveness is the key to obtaining both physical and spiritual salvation. Those who have become the children of God through the new birth have special obligations to members of God's family and to other human beings. Believers are to forgive others as God in Christ Jesus has forgiven us. Refusal to forgive makes a person unable to receive forgiveness from God. The Bible says, 'But I say unto you, Love your enemies, bless them that curse you, do good to them that hate you, and pray for them which despitefully use you, and persecute you' (Matt. 5:44).

A son is marked by obeying his father and by following his father's steps. Christian sonship means sacrificial love, loving one's enemies, and praying for one's persecutors. Does that sound too difficult for you? Remember that Jesus also prayed for his enemies while He was nailed to the tree of anguish. 'Jesus said, "Father, forgive them, for they do not know what they are doing." And they divided up his clothes by casting lots' (Luke 23:34).

This is equally required of you as a born-again Christian, if you would obtain your forgiveness. 'For if you forgive men when they sin against you, your heavenly Father will also forgive you. But if you do not forgive men their sins, your Father will not forgive your sins' (Matt. 6:14–15).

God's salvation is the cleansing of His people from their filthiness. Whenever we commit the sins of idolatry, fornication, adultery, witchcraft, and so on, we profane the name of God before the people. God will always act to defend His holy name because He wants His people to know the awesome holiness that separates Him from other gods.

God is ever determined to cleanse His people from their sins. The Bible says, 'I will sprinkle clean water on you, and you will be clean; I will cleanse you from all your impurities and from all your idols' (Ezek. 36:25).

When God forgives, He also sanctifies, to remove you from all uncleanness and fill you with His Spirit. Then restoration is guaranteed. The Bible says, 'I will give you a new heart and put a new spirit in you; I will remove from you your heart of stone and give you a heart of flesh. And I will put my Spirit in you and move you to follow my decrees and be careful to keep my laws' (Ezek. 36:26–27). 'Heaven and earth will pass away but my word shall not pass away' (Matt. 24:35).

Promise of Deliverance

From the very moment Adam and Eve ate the forbidden fruit in the garden of Eden, the perfect world was turned upside down. All perfection disappeared. Humanity was plunged into the bondage of sin and death, manifested in sickness, pain, disease, poverty, struggling, stagnation, limitation, war, and death. Man has lost grace, peace, freedom, and the presence of God.

The pronounced judgement of God over the serpent in Genesis 3:15 was inclusive of victory, deliverance, and the restoration of humanity by the Son of God, the offspring of the woman. God's covenant with Noah, Abraham, Isaac, Jacob, and David, which also manifested in Jesus Christ, contained both deliverance and restoration of man to the original form and shape described in

Genesis 1. The prophet Obadiah predicted this great heavenly warfare against the stronghold of the Devil and says, 'But on Mount Zion "church" will be deliverance, it will be holy, "sanctified" and the house of Jacob will possess their possession "restoration". Amen' (CITATION).

Isaiah predicted the mandate of deliverance of the Anointed One in chapter 61. From the beginning of Jesus's ministry to His finished work at the cross of Calvary, His ministry was deliverance.

Jesus also confirm this prediction in the temple at the beginning of His ministry (Luke 4:18–19). Jesus declared: The Spirit of the Lord is upon me, because he hath anointed me to preach the gospel to the poor, he hath sent me to heal the broken-hearted, to preach deliverance to the captives and recovering of sight to the blind, to set at liberty them that are bruised, To preach the acceptable year of the Lord.

Jesus Christ says, 'And you shall know the truth and the truth will set you free' (John 8:32). The word of God is the truth (John 17:17). Deliverance manifests in freedom for you to possess your possession and actualise your potentials. No one in captivity can succeed; it takes deliverance to obtain freedom to live.

Deliverance is the great and wonderful plan, and the expression of God's love for humanity.

I wrote extensively on the subject of deliverance in my family handbook, *Christian Marriage and Family Life*.

Promise of Restoration

Let me dedicate this segment to sharing the great and precious promises, which are our heritage in Jesus Christ. Knowing God and His Son Jesus through the Word of God makes life more exciting and fulfilling, and reveals God's wonderful plans and purposes for our lives.

The promised gift of the Holy Spirit, fulfilled on the day of Pentecost, is the ultimate restoration of age. The Bible says, 'So I will restore to you the years that the swarming locust has eaten, the crawling locust, the consuming locust, and the chewing locust, my great army which I sent among you' (Joel 2:25). This passage is a whole promise of a total recovery.

His divine power has given us everything we need for life and godliness through our knowledge of him who called us by his own glory and goodness. Through these he has given us his very great and precious promises, so that through them you may participate in the divine nature and escape the corruption in the world caused by evil desires. (2 Pet. 1:3–4)

For no matter how many promises God has made, they are 'Yes' in Christ. And so through him the 'Amen' is spoken by us to the glory of God. (2 Cor. 1:20)

Can plunder be taken from warriors or captive rescued from the fierce? But this is what the Lord say: yes, captive will be taken from warriors and plunder from retrieved from the fierce; I will contend with those who contend with you and your children I will save. (Isa. 49:24–25)

The Lord promises to help us recover everything that belongs to us, to contend with those who contend with us, and to restore all that was taken captive from us. Even mighty and terrible foes will have to release the captives when the almighty God contends with them. Amen.

That God does not leave us to our own schemes is seen in the promise to Abraham, a threefold promise of restoration, of blessing, and of land and descendants. Nevertheless, the assurance of a large family and a place for them to live is not the ultimate restoration. God's purpose is ratified in Genesis 15, marked with the sign of circumcision in chapter 17, and repeated to Isaac and Jacob in the stories that follow. It is to umpire blessing to all nations, restoring humanity to its original place, i.e., bringing humanity back to the presence of God, as it was in the garden of Eden (Rev. 21:3).

God began the process of restoration in a long story, rooted in a people and a land, in which God progressively worked out His plan of restoration. It will become clear as the story unfolds that all of human life, even creation itself, is included in its scope. God's promises to Abraham may be read in conjunction with Genesis 1 as a reaffirmation of His blessing on men and women and the whole earth.

The covenant made between God and his people provides major milestones and is key to restoration. Jesus is the key to the covenant. As Paul wrote in Galatians 3:29: 'If you belong to Christ, then you are Abraham's seed, and heirs according to the promise.' God remains to this day in the business of restoration.

New Testament Prophecy about Restoration

Restoration in each dimension of human experience is fundamental to the evangelical Christian. It is entwined in all Scripture and should be found in the entry point of our ministry of truth. Repentance is the conveyance vehicle for restoration. 'Repent, then, and turn to God. So that your sins may be wiped out, that times of refreshing may come from the Lord. And that He may send the Christ. Who has been appointed for you – even Jesus. He must remain in heaven until the time comes for God to restore everything as he promised long ago through His prophets' (Acts 3:19–21). This is the most exciting reference to restoration in the New Testament. Peter makes an urgent call to return to God to be cleansed of sin.

Our genuine return to the Lord paves the road to a period of revitalisation and revival resulting from the Lord's presence among His people. The return of Christ will be made ready, when, according to Peter, 'whom the heaven must receive (or detain) until the times of restoration of all things, of which God spoke by the mouth of his holy prophets who had been from ancient time' (Acts 3:21).

Many think that in these last days, every prophecy will be fulfilled and the restoration will be completed. The final restoration is the return of the church, which is the bride of Christ, to the majesty and glory which God had prepared for her (Matt. 24:31). For this restoration to take place, God has begun to allow His power and purity to flow without measure. 'The restoration of all things' has begun, so that the unshakable kingdom will manifest.

The scriptural definition of restoration, according to Job 42, is to re-establish something to its original condition. Therefore, when something is restored in scriptural terms, it always grows, multiplies, or improves, so that its final condition is superior to its original state (Joel 2:21–26).

For example, under the Law of Moses, if someone stole a bullock or sheep, it wasn't sufficient reparation to restore the animal he had taken. He had to pay for the equivalent of five bullocks or sheep (Exod. 22:1). When God restored Job after the terrible trials to which he was submitted, God gave him double that which he had lost and blessed him more abundantly in his final days than at the beginning of his life (Job 42:10–12). Jesus told His disciples that everyone who left something to follow him would receive one hundred times more than what was left. (Mark 10:29–30).

God multiplies when He restores; therefore, God will not only restore to the church the glory that it attained in New Testament times. He wishes to make it more powerful, glorious, and majestic, like nothing the world has ever seen!

The Bible says:

This is what the Lord Almighty says, In a little while, I will once more shake the heavens and the earth. The sea and the dry land, I will shake all nations and the desired of all nations will comes. And I will fill this house with glory say the Lord Almighty. The glory of this present house will be greater than the glory of the former house says the Lord Almighty. And in this place I will grant peace, declares the Lord Almighty. (Hag. 2:6–9)

Restoration in the Beginning

The biblical theme of restoration is found in the beginning of all things: the book of Genesis. God created human beings male and female. They enjoyed God's image and likeness unsought, including an uninterrupted relationship with Him.

However, human beings decided to eat of the forbidden fruit. By doing so, man took life in his own hands. Instead of depending on God's presence and divine provision (grace), humanity would live by their own limited resources, according to their own opinions. With this tragic decision, human beings lost the divine image and likeness of God, as well as the fellowship and companionship of the Lord.

But God's restorative plan and work began immediately (Gen. 3:15). As humans were already self-conscious, trying to cover their nakedness by their own hands, God provided them clothes made of animal skins. This revealed with complete clarity God's redemptive and restorative plan for fallen humanity. This first sacrifice, which provided humans with clothes, pointed toward the final sacrifice of Jesus, the Lamb of God.

After mankind was expelled from the garden of Eden, separating them from the Tree of Life which was in its midst, they rushed to degradation (Gen. 6:5). Adam had sons in his own image and likeness, disobedient and self-centred, and not in God's image and likeness (Genesis 5:3). From that moment forward, human beings fell further and further into iniquity, until God decided to destroy His entire creation and begin again with Noah's family.

The covenant of the rainbow in Genesis 9 was one of the most important signs given by God during this period, a sign through which His desire to restore that which had been lost in Adam and Eve's time was indicated. In Genesis 12, God began to develop His plan and purpose of salvation through one person, Abraham.

God gave Abraham a promise of a great and prosperous nation that began to gestate as Israel, but was destined to be transformed into the church, the house of God. Although there are many prophecies dedicated to Israel, we can be assured that from the beginning, God had the church in His heart as the means through which to implement the restorative plan for fallen humanity.

The anticipated restoration was brilliantly demonstrated in the life of Joseph, who was hated, abandoned in the cistern, sold into slavery, falsely accused, jailed, and forgotten. But he finally became favoured by God and restored to the role God assigned for him (Gen. 41:42–43).

When humans failed at self-restoration in Jeremiah 8, God promised to send a prophet like Moses to the Israelites in order to guarantee their freedom. It was for this reason that they refused to listen to God, and insisted that God should speak directly only to Moses (Deut. 18:15–16). Their fear of hearing directly from God without intermediaries placed them under the Law, under which humans struggle to obtain and retain divine favour. But God, knowing the limits of the Law, instituted the Mosaic system of animal sacrifices to atone for sins. He also converted the Law into a demonstration that pointed to definitive salvation through the shed blood of Jesus Christ, the sacrifice made once for all (Heb. 10:10).

Failure human efforts at self-restoration are explicitly presented in Jeremiah 8 and Lamentations 2, in the destruction of Jerusalem and dispersion of the people. These chapters paint a picture of human foolishness, rebellion, immorality, idolatry, and general corruption exhibited by the nation of Israel, forcing God to discipline them in such a manner that 'he came to be like an enemy' (Lam. 2:5).

Jeremiah 9 summarizes their difficult situation, which mirrors the activities of many in today's church: 'And they have not known me' (v. 3). In spite of God's great insistence, human beings still have not established a personal relationship with God.

Corruption and Restoration of Leaders

Obligated to listen to others in place of God, the people began to listening to liars (Jer. 9:3). Ezekiel 34 exposes the weakness and depravity into which the Jewish leaders fell. They used their offices and ministries for personal gain instead of serving the people. They didn't feed the flock but themselves, as it is in today's churches. In His wrath, God confronted these evil shepherds, warning them that He would take the sheep away from them and put an end to their exploitation.

The resemblance of the pastor is maintained in the promise of restoration that follows these sentences of divine disapproval: 'Behold, I myself will go seek my sheep ... As the flock recognizes the shepherd ... thus will I recognize my sheep' (Ezek. 34:11, 12). God often wishes that His people would relate directly to

Him, hear Him, respond to Him, and have a more abundant life. The Lord has never turned away from His promise to restore the loving relationship that was lost in the garden of Eden.

Restoration and the Futility of Ritual Religion

As humanity has always sought to gain God's acceptance through its own efforts, so human beings have always fashioned the pattern of their relationship with God. They often think that observing certain rules and regulations, practicing certain doctrines, and pronouncing some set words can retain God's favour and salvation. But Jesus said all who worship His Father worship Him in Spirit and truth (John 4:24).

The Lord makes it clear through the messages of the prophets that those concepts are in error. He despises worship rituals and formal sacrifices (Amos 5:21–22), and ridicules solemnities (Isa. 58:4–5) and lip service (Jer. 7:4–7). He rejects their songs in which they intone praises that mean nothing to them (Amos 5:23). He promises to convert their songs into lamentations, to transform their voices into cries of grief (Jer. 7:34).

Removal of Human Works

At that time, His voice shook the earth, but now he has promised, 'once more I will shake not only the earth but also the heaven' (CITATION). The words 'once more' indicate the removal of things that can be shaken–in other words created things – so that what cannot be shaken may remain (Heb. 12:26–27). All that Israel and Judah had built for themselves by their own effort for generations was abomination to God, and He handed everything over for destruction (Jer.1:16; 32:29–36).

This message about the Israelites' false beliefs and doctrines extends to today's churches. Hence, the author of Hebrews speaks of the removal that God plans to bring to pass in our lives, and particularly in the church, to allow for perfect restoration (Heb. 12:26–27). He has promised to remove every human work built up by the energy and wisdom of the flesh. Only the unshakable things which have been built by the wisdom and eternal power of the Lord will remain.

The great removal prophesied in Hebrews has begun, and will continue in the church. This is because, due to the same evils that affected Israel – seeking to please God through ritual worship; idolatrous practices and moral decadence; corruption of the leadership; and worshipping the work of human hands, which are also manifesting in the church today –removal forms part of the process of restoration.

Repentance Is an Act of Restoration

After the judgement and discipline of the people for their apostasy, i.e., abandoning the faith which they had professed to observe, God offers them wonderful promises of restoration. He tells them that their salvation will soon be allowed to come to pass, that it will be 'like a watered garden'. He will free them from their iniquities, heal their apostasies, and love them 'out of pure grace' (Isa. 58; Jer. 31–33; Ezek. 36:22– 38).

Nevertheless, in their warnings about justice in God's promise of restoration, the prophets of God make an important exhortation:

'Repent! Abandon your ritual fasting and practice true fasting' (Isa. 58). Repentance doesn't mean to redouble your efforts to please God by keeping the Law or achieving good works. The calling has always been to simply return to God or obey the commandment of God, to allow Him to cleanse and restore you as a sinner.

Restoration of the Tabernacle of David

In Acts 15:1–29, the question arises of whether Gentiles can be accepted as Christians without submitting to the Law of Moses? Peter responded that neither the Jews nor their fathers had been able to support the weight of the Law; therefore, they should not ask the Gentiles to submit to it. 'On the contrary, we believe that through the grace of our Lord Jesus Christ we are saved, so also the Gentiles' (v. 11). James confirmed Peter's declaration, citing the passage in Amos in which God promised to rebuild 'the tabernacle of David ... that the rest of men might seek the Lord' (vv. 16, 17).

The tabernacle of David is mentioned in many other places in Scripture, although this name is not always used. Frequently 'Zion' is used, the mountain of Jerusalem on which sits the tabernacle where God dwells alongside His people.

Joel 2 begins with an emotional calling: 'Play the trumpet in Zion, and sound an alarm in my holy mountain.' Hebrews 12:22 says, 'You must come to Mount Zion.' In both cases, the reference is to the tabernacle of David. An understanding of the concept of the divine restoration of that tabernacle is essential, because it allows a clear biblical vision of the church today.

Origin and description of the Tabernacle of David

The tabernacle of David was established shortly after David succeeded Saul as king. The ark of the covenant, which represented the presence and power of God, had been captured by the Philistines. After a series of plagues, they returned it to Kirjath-jearim, and from there it was brought to the house of Abinidab (1 Sam. 4:1–7). David yearned to have it by his side and near the people of Israel, so that God's presence would be manifested. He had the ark returned to Jerusalem, placing it in a tent on Mount Zion (2 Sam. 6; 1 Chron. 13:16).

Before its capture, the ark had been situated in the tabernacle of Moses, resting in the most sacred Holy of Holies. Only the high priest could come near it to sprinkle its cover once a year with the blood of a sacrificed animal (Heb. 9:1–7). The people could only approach the outer part of the tabernacle in order to present their sacrifices and worship God.

The tabernacle of David marked a revolutionary change in this practice of separating the people from God. Without violating the spirit of the Law of Moses, David cultivated intimate relationships between the people and their Lord with praise and worship.

The great significance of the tabernacle rested on the fact that the ark was the representative of God's presence, occupying a central place among the people of Jerusalem. David taught the people to worship God with praises, thanksgiving, and rejoicing. Some sixteen ministers were ordained to cover the twenty-four hours of the day, seven days a week. None of them were associated with guilt or condemnation; they all expressed recognition of God's grace and mercy, and their unconditional acceptance of all who approached Him with faith.

The restoration of the tabernacle of David nowadays means to discard formality, legalism, and condemnation, bringing the suffering people of the church and the world back into the arms of a loving God (Heb. 10:1–25). The Lord invites all to return to Him, to cast their sins behind them, and to receive the refreshing that comes from being in His presence (Acts 3:19).

Restoration of the Image of God

Just as the tabernacle of David represents the restoration of fellowship with God that was lost in the garden of Eden, renovation symbolizes the restoration of God's image and likeness – holiness and family ties with God. Isaiah 4 speaks of the renovation of the tabernacle which will flourish in the future. The renewal is Christ, who is the Head of the true church. The true church is composed of those who have received salvation and the new birth by grace. Jesus identified Himself with the vine, and His disciples with the branches, and said that they would bear much fruit if they remained in Him (John 15:5).

In many other places, the Scriptures denote that, in Jesus Christ, God restores His people to the Father-son ties that were broken by Adam's disobedience. All those who believe in Him are returned to God's house (Eph. 2:19) and conformed to his image (Rom. 8:29).

Restoration of Fellowship with God

The Lord illustrates the restoration of relationship with His people through the image of the Bridegroom and His bride. The passage in Revelation 19 describes the wedding of the Lamb, when Jesus calls His bride once she's ready to be presented before Him. In the letter to the Ephesians, Paul explains how the bride is prepared: submitting herself to God and allowing Him to cleanse her 'in the washing of water by the Word', in order to present her before the Lord without 'stain or wrinkle or any such thing' (Eph. 5:25–27).

When the bride, the church, is prepared and Jesus returns for her, the broken relationship between God and man in the garden of Eden will be restored completely. Christians will become one in Christ and God, fulfilling Jesus's prayers in John 17. As in the first marriage, the spouse will be the bone of His bones and flesh of His flesh, completely like Him. The Lord will not return for an impure or defeated wife. In these days of restoration, God prepares the wife in beauty and power and His visible glory.

Holy Spirit: Agent of Restoration

God's work of restoration is performed through the Holy Spirit and through the lives of those who have believed in Jesus and been born again from on high (John 3:3). The prophet Joel prophesied about God pouring out His Spirit 'upon all flesh' (Joel 2:28, 29). In this way, His power would be received by all and would not be limited to a special individual. This explains why Christ said to His disciples that it was necessary that He go to the Father (John 16:7). Only then would the Holy Spirit be sent to dwell in them, to fill them, so that God's wonders would be performed through them.

Titus 3 reveals that even salvation, which is the regeneration of the Holy Spirit dwelling in human beings and the cleansing that makes this new creature acceptable before God, is the work of the Holy Spirit.

Finally, in Acts 1:8, Jesus tells the disciples that they may do nothing until the Holy Spirit comes. The Lord promises that they will receive power to testify about Him and to spread the truth of the gospel to all the earth, from Jerusalem to Judea, from Samaria to the uppermost part of the world.

Significance of Restoration for the Individual

Conceivably, the best way to sum up all that the restoration means to the individual believer is to call on a simple word used as much in the Old Testament as in the new life. In Deuteronomy 30:20, Moses says of the Lord, 'He is life for you'. In Colossians 3:4, Paul speaks of 'Christ, our life'. And Jesus says, 'I have come to give them life, and so that they may have it in abundance' (John 10:10).

Restoration, for the individual, means to replace spiritual death with spiritual life. Ezekial 36 graphically describes that substitution. However, we not only receive a new quality of life, but we should also grow in it. In many verses, we see this process of growth reflected as a work of the Holy Spirit (John 16:23; 17:22; Rom. 8:13). Through the Holy Spirit, God is consistently perfecting the work for our salvation.

Significance of Restoration for the Church

Remember that, for God, 'restoration' means the creation of something that surpasses the original. For the church as a whole, restoration signifies something more than being converted into the new-image church of Christ.

In the first place, restoration means that the church will deploy the type of love that Jesus manifested during His earthly ministry. Jesus said that people would know His disciples by their love (John 13:34–35). Restoration also means the manifestation of God's unlimited power through His church. It should occur when the gifts of the Spirit flow through the people of God, who work without limitations and restrictions under the direction of the Holy Spirit.

Through the full manifestation of the gifts and ministries marked out by God, and working according to the love essential to His divine nature, the church will reach a level of maturity that can only be measured in terms of the 'measure of the stature of the fullness of Christ' (Eph. 4:13). The church will be converted into a holy temple (Eph. 2:21), inhabited by a consecrated priesthood which offers acceptable sacrifices to God through Jesus Christ (1 Pet. 2:5). All people will be drawn to the Lord, and the world will finally see God's glory through this restored church.

The Gifts of the Spirit

Since the Holy Spirit is the agent of restoration, it is therefore very important to know how He distributes His gifts to individuals so that the works of restoration and perfection can be established in the church. The apostle Paul wrote to the Corinthians on this very important subject thus: 'Now about spiritual gifts, brethren's, I do not want you to be ignorant' (1 Cor. 12:1).

God poured out His Spirit on the church in the day of Pentecost (Acts 2:1–4). From that time, all believers in Christ have continued to receive the baptism of the Holy Spirit. In Corinth, some Christian were unclear about this, because some church members spoke in unknown tongues, enabled by the Holy Spirit (1 Cor. 14:2). Paul explained this was a gift from the Holy Spirit. It worked to extend the gospel message in a church which knew the way of love; was active when the church used His spirit of prophecy to proclaim the gospel; and manifested when people confessed that Jesus is the Lord.

Paul listed nine gifts given to some of God's people so they could carry out responsibilities for human restoration. These gifts vary from person to person.

The nine gifts are word of knowledge, word of wisdom, faith, healing, miracle power, prophecy, discerning spirit, speaking in tongues, and interpretation of tongues. (Paul did not mention the gifts of music, praise and worship here.)

The Holy Spirit Himself is the ultimate spiritual gift. His most characteristic work is to give selected individuals gifts with which to serve God by serving the people. The Holy Spirit always brings one or more spiritual gifts to a believer. These gifts are spiritual talents or spiritual endowments which equip a person to serve Christ diligently. Anyone who uses a gift to create disunity among God's people is misguided. Gifts are for the building up of the entire church, not for making people feel proud.

The Fivefold Church Government Offices

'He said therefore, A certain nobleman went into a far country to receive for himself a kingdom and to return. And he called his ten servants, and delivered them ten pounds. And said unto them, Occupy till I come' (Luke 19:12-13).

The fivefold ministry offices are stewardship that demands for our commitment and dedication to the works of the kingdom, for which we shall all be held accountable and rewarded.

The unity of the Trinity in the work of restoration through the church is emphasised in the function of the fivefold ministries. God's plan is to create a great family of free persons to be His own people. Paul exhorted Christians to keep the unity of the Spirit through the bond of peace (Eph. 4:3).

Jesus is the One who came from heaven to the earth, and also ascended back to heaven with resurrected power, capturing all evil powers. Jesus sent the Holy Spirit back to the earth. The ascended Lord did not forget the church and the people He left behind. He sent the Holy Spirit with fivefold gifts to equip His church for ministry, namely apostle, prophet, evangelist, pastor, and teacher (Eph. 4:11).

These fivefold ministries are covenant offices. One is appointed to these offices purely at the discretion of our Lord Jesus Christ, who is the Head of the church, and the Holy Spirit, who is the abiding God. 'You did not choose me, but I chose you to go and bear fruit, fruit that will abide' (John 15:16). Anyone appointed to these offices is a minister or an ambassador of Jesus Christ, serving for the purpose of equipping believers to do the works of the ministry and to build up the church. The goal of Jesus Christ is that such equipping, ministering, and building will go on until maturity into full stature of Christ is achieved before His return.

Let me mention briefly the mode of operation of the fivefold ministries:

1. *Apostle* or *apostolos* in the Greek language means an envoy, ambassador, messenger, or missionary, with the mandate to cultivate new land for the church – planting, and nurturing the church. The name 'apostle' appears in New Testament seventy-nine times: ten times in the Gospels, twenty-eight time in Acts. thirty-eight times in the Epistles, and three times in Revelation.

2. *Prophets* are the mouthpieces of God, appointed to speak the word of knowledge to declare what God is about to do. Prophets also serves as counsellors. God often sends them as His ambassadors to nations, kings, and kingdoms, including individuals. Prophets reproach, correct, and redeem lost souls.

3. *Evangelists* are defined as those seeking to convert others to Christian faith by public preaching. Evangelists function as gospel singers, authors of Christian books and journals, and media personalities in radio and television evangelism. Evangelists carry the anointing for the Great Commission (Matt. 28:19–20; Mark 16:15–18).

4. *Pastors* or shepherds are directly responsible for church administration, nurturing and feeding the flock of God with the Word of God. Pastors carry the hearts of shepherds, leading the flock to greener pasture for feeding, and beside the still water to quench their thirst. Jesus called Peter three times and said to him, 'Feed my sheep' (John 21:17).

   Whoever wants to be a pastor must also be a teacher of the Word of God.

5. *Teachers* teach the Word of God with in-depth revelation knowledge. Paul admonished Timothy, his spiritual son, thus: 'Study to show thyself approved unto God a workman that needed not be ashamed but rightly dividing (teaching) the word of truth' (2 Tim. 2:15). All ministers of God – apostles, prophets, evangelists, and pastors – are expected to be teachers of the Word of God.

The fivefold ministries are offices with specific portfolios, each for the building of the church to the full stature of our Lord Jesus Christ. They are not promotional titles.

The Promise of Healing and Longevity

Beloved, remember that death has no power over the life of believers because of the sacrifice and victory of the cross. All you need to do is to grab and appropriate the Word of God into every situations in your life. Read them over and over again. *Speak these words out loudly.* There is something powerful about audibly speaking God's Word!

Death and Life are in the power of the tongue: and they that love it shall eat the fruit thereof. (Prov. 18:21)

I am the living One; I was dead, and behold, I am alive forever and ever! And hold the keys of death and Hades. (Rev. 1:18)

Believe the Scriptures that you will find throughout this chapter. They will not fail you if you trust and obey God's Word. The keys are *trust* and *obey*, to allow God to do it in His own way and in His time. It will all come out okay, because God wants to help us out of our sickness and diseases.

Here are the wonderful healing promises that can be found in the Scripture:

Behold, the eye of the Lord is upon them that fear Him, upon them that hope in His mercy; to deliver their soul from death, and to keep them alive in famine. Our soul waited for the Lord; He is our help and our shield. For our heart shall rejoice in Him, because we have trusted in His holy Name. Let thy mercy, O LORD, be upon us, according as we hope in Thee. (Ps. 33:18–22)

Remember that you need to ask God for the anointing of the Holy Spirit and let the Word of God be engrafted in your heart with faith to obtain your healing. It takes the Spirit of God and the Word working together for the miracle of healing to manifest. Don't leave the Holy Spirit out! Ask for His presence while praying for healing.

God's Word tells us that the Word itself is a seed that can bring life and health to your whole being.

Trust in the Word and Promises of God

My son, attend to my words; incline thine ear unto my sayings. Let them not depart from thine eyes; keep them in the midst of thine heart. For they are LIFE unto those that find them, and HEALTH to all their flesh. Keep thy heart with all diligence; for out of it are the issues of life. (Prov. 4:20–23)

The Word of God cannot be broken. God created and sustained the universe with His Word.

Through him (The WORD), all things were made; without him (The WORD) nothing was made that has been made. In him (The WORD) was life, and that life was the light of men. (John. 1:3–4)

You will never be disappointed if you allow the Word of God to rule your life as a born-again child of God.

He sent His word and healed them, and delivered them from their destructions. (Ps. 107:20)

I am the Lord that healeth thee. (Exod. 15:26)

God is not a man, that he should lie; neither the son of man, that he should repent: hath he said, and shall he not done it? Or hath he spoken, and shall he not make it good? (Num. 23:19)

There hath not failed one word of all His good promise. (1 Kgs 8:56)

For ever O, Lord, thy word is settled in heaven. (Ps. 119:89)

I will hasten my Word to perform it. (Jer. 1:12)

God Almighty declared Himself the Healer of His people with these words. He spoke those words to over a million people in Exodus 12. After all the plagues that fell upon Egypt, they believed that God's words were true. The result was that every one of the Israelites who needed healing were made whole in preparation for the trip to the Promised Land.

This was confirmed in Psalm 105, where we are told that 'He (God) brought them forth ... and there was not one feeble person among their tribes' (v. 37). Nobody limped out of Egypt! Nobody was carried on a stretcher! The Lord healed them, perhaps on that Passover night.

This wonderful miracle work of God inspired Moses to write:

If you pay attention to these laws and are careful to follow them, then the Lord your God will keep his covenant of love with you ... The Lord will keep you free from EVERY DISEASE. He will not inflict on you the horrible diseases you knew in Egypt, but he will inflict them on all who hate you. (Deut. 7:12–15)

But you shall serve the Lord your God, and He will bless your bread and your water; and He will remove sickness from your midst. (Exod. 23:25)

If that was true in Israel, under the Law, should it not be much more true for us under the grace of Jesus Christ? Jesus was known as teacher and healer. His healing miracles attracted suffering people, and He compassionately ministered healing to all who were sick among His audience.

Trust in the Word and Promises of God

Jesus Christ welcomed them (the crowds) and spoke to them about the kingdom of God, and healed those who needed healing. (Luke 9:11)

News about Him spread all over Syria, and people brought to him all who were ill with various diseases, those suffering severe pain, the demon possessed, those having seizures, and the paralysed, and he healed them. (Matt. 4:24)

Remember that God created you perfectly, without any form of sickness or disease, until the Devil came to defile you. The grace of God has brought Jesus to deliver mankind from the captivity of Satan.

Lo, I come, to do thy will, O God. (Heb. 10:7)

I (Jesus) came down from heaven, not to do mine own will, but the will of him that sent me. (John 6:38)

[The Leper said:] 'If you are willing, you can make me clean.' Filled with compassion, Jesus reached out his hand and touched the man. 'I am willing,' he said, 'Be clean!' (Mark 1:40)

Remember that the same Jesus who healed all manner of sicknesses and diseases 2,015 years ago is alive forever and still doing the same job. He does so through His Word and the Holy Spirit, by the anointed men and women of God.

Is anyone among you sick? Let him call for the elders (saintly leaders) of the church, and let them pray over him, anointing him with oil in the name of the Lord; and the prayer offered in faith will restore the one who is sick, and the Lord will raise him up, and if he has committed sins, they will be forgiven him.

Therefore, confess your sins to one another, and pray for one another, so that you may be healed. The effective prayer of a righteous man can accomplish much. (Jas. 5:14–16)

Jesus's salvation was perfectly balanced. He provided for the well-being of humanity's spiritual, emotional, and physical needs.

Great multitudes followed him (Jesus), and he healed them ALL. (Matt. 12:15)

As many as touched the hem of his garment were made perfectly whole. (Matt. 14:36)

Jesus used all means to help people in their various needs and point them to their greatest need, which is salvation. Jesus's love and healing resulted in the news about Him spreading all over. Large crowds followed Him. It wasn't some who touched Him that received healing, but 'as many as touched Him'. Anyone and everyone who needed healing received it when they touched the Master.

The whole multitude sought to touch him; (and He) healed them ALL. (Luke 6:19)

And Jesus went about all the cities and villages, teaching in their synagogues, and preaching the gospel of the kingdom, and healing every sickness and every diseases among the people. (Matt. 9:35)

He ... healed ALL that were sick: that it might be fulfilled which was spoken by Isaiah the prophet, saying, Himself took OUR infirmities, and bare our sicknesses. (Matt. 8:16–17)

Beloved, Jesus Christ is the same forever (Heb. 13:8). Believers have no excuse to return to inferior religion. Our Saviour is eternal and consistent. We can always count on Him for our spiritual, emotional, psychological, and physical healing. God says, 'My covenant will I not break, nor alter the thing that is gone out of my lips' (Ps. 89:34). You have been given a name that is greater than all names, that at the mention of the name of Jesus Christ, every knee shall bow.

The same authority that came to the disciples after the baptism of Holy Spirit on the day of Pentecost is equally available to you forever. Whenever you decree and declare your healing in faith and in the name of Jesus Christ, surely, it shall be established.

I shall not die, but live, and declare the works of the LORD. (Ps. 118:17)

O Lord my God, I called to YOU for help and YOU healed me. O Lord, you brought me up from the grave; you spared me from going down into the pit. (Ps. 30:2–3)

I am the resurrection and the life, he who believes in me will live, even though he dies, and whoever lives and believes in me will never die.

Do you believe this? You faith is critical to your healing. If you believe, you will see the glory of God.

For the Lord takes pleasure in His people; He will beautify the afflicted ones with SALVATION. (Ps. 149:4)

Declare your own healing as an anointed one, to establish your healing.

Heal me, O Lord, and I will be healed; save me and I will be saved, for you are the one I praise. (Jer. 17:14)

[Jesus said to His disciples:] When you enter a town ... heal the sick who are there and tell them, 'The kingdom of God is near you.' (Luke 10:9)

Jesus has given us the authority through the anointing of Holy Spirit to heal the sick and preach the good news! Anyone can preach a sermon or give a talk, but only those truly anointed can pray for the sick and see God healing them. I pray that God will anoint you with the power to heal the sick. In Jesus's name, amen.

Surely he (Jesus) took up our infirmities and carried our sorrows ... By his wounds we ARE healed. (Isa. 53:4–5)

Whatsoever you shall ask the Father in my name, he will give it you. (John 16:23)

What - so - ever 'things' you desire, when you pray, believe that you receive them, and you shall have them. (Mark 11:24)

He (God the Father) that spared not His own Son (Jesus), but delivered HIM up (to be nailed on the Cross) for us all, how shall HE (God the Father) not with Him (Jesus) also freely give us all things? (Rom. 8:32)

Our God is a super Father, above all human fathers, who wants to give His children those good things that will meet our needs for abundant life, now and forever. Healing is not a gift that would spoil us like riches, luxury cars and jewellery. Some earthly parents shower their children with expensive presents that ruin the child. Such gifts are evil things. But our God wants to give us health that we might shine for Him in a more glorious way.

The Lord not only wants to heal you of the big diseases, but He wants to heal you of the aches, the pains, the colds, and the flu too.

And when Jesus was come into Peter's house, he saw his wife's mother laid, and sick of a fever. And he touched her hand, and the fever left her: and she arose, and ministered unto them. (Matt. 8:14–15)

If two of you shall agree on earth as touching or concerning anything that they shall ask, it shall be done for them of my Father which is in heaven. (Matt. 18:19)

God's healing of a broken body or a broken spirit is a pure request that two Christians can agree on with God and know that He desires to bring it to pass in His way and in His time.

One of God's names in the Old Testament Hebrew is Jehovah-Rapha (Exod. 15:26). This name translates as 'God the healer'. His name is Healer because healing is part of His very nature.

Bless the Lord, O my soul; And all that is within me, bless His holy name. Bless the Lord, O my soul, And forget none of His benefits; Who pardons ALL your iniquities; Who heals ALL your diseases; Who redeems your life from the pit; Who crowns you with loving-kindness and compassion; Who satisfies your years with good things, So that your youth is renewed like the eagle. (Ps. 103:1–5)

Brothers, sisters, and beloved in Christ, you can get your youth renewed in healing if only you believe and act accordingly. You need to be healed to run and not get tired, to walk and not faint.

Note that in God's perspective, with the death of our Lord Jesus Christ on the cross, you have already received healing of your pain, sickness, and disease. All you need is to stand up in faith and claim your heritage in Christ Jesus.

Sometimes healing comes instantly, like the miracle at the Beautiful Gate. When healing is instantaneous, that is what the Bible reveals to be a miracle, sign, and wonder. However, more often than not, healing comes by degrees.

Healing is guaranteed absolutely for believers.

For this corruptible must put on incorruptible, and this mortal must put on immortality. So when this corruptible shall have put on incorruptible, and this mortal shall have put on immortality, then shall be brought to pass the saying that is written, Death is swallowed up in victory. (1 Cor. 15:53–54)

In fact healing is already granted and is already ours. We simply need to pray it into our lives and thank God for healing in advance.

Jesus even healed sinners! The man who had been crippled for thirty-eight years, whom Jesus made whole, was told by Jesus to go and sin no more, that nothing worse come upon him (John 5:14).

The more we give ourselves to personal sanctification, obedient to God's commands, the more we'll experience healing power.

These two doctrines walk alongside each other. The more the Spirit of God lives and acts in the soul of believers, the more miracles will multiply by which He works in the body.

If my people who are called by my name will humble themselves and pray and seek my face and turn from their wicked ways, then will I hear from heaven and will forgive their sin and will heal their land. (2 Chron. 7:14)

This is a principle and teaching of the highest import for divine healing.

Heaven and earth shall pass away, but my word will not pass away. (Matt. 24:35)

Promises of Blessing and Prosperity

The faithfulness of God is exhibited in His desire to bless humanity. This is stated in Genesis 1:28 and demonstrated in the content of all Scripture. The cost of following the way of faith in the Lord includes unselfish service, sacrifice, and offering. A line of sacred empowerment can be observed from Abraham to the apostles. The treasure of God's blessings is prepared for his dedicated and obedient children and servants. He has promised blessing, prosperity, and abundance.

Faithfulness in offering, tithe, and service are repaid with abundance, blessing, and prosperity when carefully maintained as written in divine law.

Divine Law of Blessing and Prosperity

One of the strategies of the Enemy is to plague humanity with financial handicap in order to paralyse our potential. This must be resisted by total obedience to the law of divine blessings and prosperity, as directed by God Himself in Scripture.

Will a man rob God? Yet you rob me. "But you ask, how do we rob you? "In tithes and offering. You are under a curse, the whole nation of you because you are robbing me. Bring the whole tithe into the storehouse that there may be food in my house. Test me in this, says the Lord Almighty, and see if I will not throw open the floodgates of heaven and pour out so much blessing that you will not have room enough for it. I will prevent pests from devouring your crops, and the vines in your fields will not cast their fruit says the Lord Almighty. Then all the nation will call you blessed for yours will be a delightful land, says the Lord Almighty. (Mal 3:8–12)

Here is the only scriptural passage where God directs human beings to test Him with their tithes and offering. Unfortunately, many are giving their offering and tithes to God as if they are giving to beggars. They murmur and grumble, saying, 'If we give now, it will end up in the account of the pastor or the elders of the church.' Many go as far as lying to God in the calculation of how much to pay. All what we end up doing by this is breaking the law of prosperity.

Give and it shall be giving unto you, good measure, pressed down, shaken together and running over, shall men give to your bosom. For with the same measure that ye mete withal, it shall be measured to you again. (Luke 6:38)

To neglect tithing and offering is to rob God, in turn robbing ourselves and renouncing God's blessings.

Many people are financially handicapped by poverty, and this is often caused by their disobedience to the Word of God in tithing and offering. This disobedience manifests in many ways. One of them is stealing from God. This passage clearly tells us that those who retain their tithes and offerings are stealing from God. In consequence, they also deprive themselves of the blessings that God wants to grant them. When a person ceases tithing, that person is violating the Law. If one violates the Law, then it can't work in one's favour.

Wise believers should not allow anything to stop them from giving offering, paying their tithing correctly, and giving seed sacrifice. This is the height of the law of blessing and prosperity. However, no one should pay tithes or offering with the objective of obtaining something. Rather, the action of giving offering and tithes must emanate from obedience to the commandment of God, as God always rewards obedience.

Malachi 3 demonstrates the power of releasing our hands with our money in order to watch the Lord perform His miraculous provision. He said, 'Bring me your tithes and offerings into the temple and I will open the windows of heaven to pour out a blessing so great, you won't have room enough to receive it.; The Lord not only promises His blessing on His people, He challenges us to prove Him and put Him to the test.

The word 'tithe' is taken from the Greek and means 'tenth'. Thus, we are blessed with ninety per cent of our income and should give ten per cent back to the Lord. God is not short of wealth that He must rely on His people to contribute. Rather, it is His intelligent plan to share in a cycle of blessing. We give to advance the work of His kingdom on earth according to the law of divine returns (Luke 6:38).

Give to God and God will give back to you. Prosperity begins with an investment – investment in the things of God. There is a universal law of divine reciprocation. You give; God gives to you. When you sow a seed, the land offers a harvest. That is a reciprocal relationship. The land gives to you if you give to the land. You deposit money in the bank and the bank pays you interest. This is called reciprocation.

However, there are many people who wish to receive without giving anything back, especially when dealing with the things of God. They know that reciprocation is fundamental in the system of the world, but they always expect God to send them something when they refuse to invest in the kingdom of God. 'You must partner with God with your life and substances in tithe and offering.'

If you are not investing your time, your talent, your dedication, and your money, why should you expect to receive something? How can you harvest when you haven't sown any seed? How can you expect God to honour your desires when you have not honoured His commandment of giving? Prosperity begins with investment.

The most profound expression of the love of God for humanity is giving and offering. It started at the beginning of life, when God created all things perfectly and gave His Spirit and dominion to man to rule over all creation. He climaxed the acts of giving when He gave His Son to be our Saviour. Giving is the character of God, to demonstrate His love for humanity. He seeks to give Himself away as a sacrifice for our redemption.

God also expects reciprocation from man. 'For God so loved the world that He gave His only begotten Son that whoever believes in Him shall not perish but have eternal life' (John 3:16).

My experience as the son of a farmer gave me a wider and deeper knowledge of planting seeds and harvesting. In the early part of my life, I enjoyed going to the farm with my parents to participate in farming, particularly during planting and harvesting seasons. My interest was to plant and watch how the seeds that were planted would germinate and bear fruit ripe enough to be harvested. It was amazing to see that a seed of maize or beans could eventually grow to bear so many more seeds – sometimes more than a thousand.

It was also amazing to find out that when a seed of orange, mango, cocoa, palm cannel, or apple is planted, it grows to become a tree that bears much fruit day after day, year after year, for human consumption. Most of these plants last from one generation to another. This is how it is when you sow your seeds of sacrifice on the altar of God.

The Bible says, 'The days are coming declares the Lord, when the reaper will be overtaken by the ploughmen and the planter by the one treading grapes. New wine will drip from the mountains and flow from all the hills' (Amos 9:13).

Our Lord Jesus Christ spoke about sowing seed in parable thus:

Then he told them many things in parables, saying: A farmer went out to sow his seed. As he was scattering the seed, some fell along the path, and the birds came and ate it up. Some fell on rocky places, where it did not have much soil. It sprang up quickly because the soil was shallow but when the sun came up, the plants were scorched, and they withered because they had no root. Other seed fell among the thorns, which grew up and shocked the plants. Still other seed fell on good soil, where they produced a crop a hundred, sixty or thirty times what was sown. He, who has ears, let him hear. (Matt. 13: 1–9)

The Word of God is the good seed. The question we need to ask ourselves is, am I a rocky, shallow, weedy, or fertile soil? Am I fertile enough to receive and sustain God's blessing?

In other words, our God-given lives and wealth are seeds. Do you sow your seed in rocky, shallow, weedy, or fertile soil? Where you sow your seed determines your blessings. Are you truly sowing the seed of your life to Christ? Do you sow the seed of your wealth to provoke God's blessing into your life, as Abraham did? Or you are sowing sparingly?

Jesus sowed His life to produce the covenant blood of redemption, by which He purchased man back to God. He rose from death to ascend into glory and is seated at the right hand of God the Father, on His throne. He declared, 'Whoever finds his life will lose it, and whoever loses his life for my sake will find it' (Matt. 13:39).

The root path to blessing and prosperity is to give your life and your belongings unsparingly to God, who is the fountain of life. The law of increase demands a release. 'Give and it shall be given unto you; good measure, pressed down and shaken together, and running over, shall men giving into your bosom. For with the same measure that ye mete withal it shall be measured to you again' (Luke 6:38).

The Sowers: Cain and Abel

The Bible tells us quite clearly that human beings originally worshipped the one true God. Cain and Abel brought their gift offerings to the Lord. They had been taught by their parents the importance of honouring God with their sacrificial offerings. 'In the course of time, Cain brought some of the fruits of the soil as an offering to the Lord. But Abel brought fat portions from the firstborn of his flock, the Lord looked with favour on his offering. But on Cain and his offering he did not look with favour' (Gen. 4:3–5).

The brothers brought gifts that were in line with their respective occupations. Cain offered a sacrifice from his vegetable and fruit harvest, and Abel as a shepherd brought a fat offering from his flock.

The important lesson in this first scripturally recorded gift offering is that God accepted Abel and his offering and did not recognise Cain and his sacrificial offering. Why was Cain's offering rejected and his brother's offering accepted? This is not an academic question but a crucially important lesson for worshippers. There is a right and wrong way to worship and give offering to God.

In the case of Cain, there was rejection of both the person and the offering. Something was certainly wrong. Abel, who was

Adam's second son, offered first-born animals to the Lord, while Cain, who was the first-born son, offered neither firstlings nor first fruits. God loves a cheerful giver who gives unsparingly.

What do you give, and what is the state of your mind as you give?

Noah's Sacrificial Offering

Noah's sacrificial offering on the first day in the new world after the flood was a special day. It was a day of worship and sacrifice to the Lord by Noah and his entire household to mark a new era. 'Then Noah built an altar to the Lord and taking some of all the clean animals and clean birds, he sacrificed burnt offerings on it' (Gen. 8:20).

Noah's gratitude was expressed by offering something very valuable to the Lord, and God responded with an everlasting covenant: 'The Lord smelled the pleasing aroma and said in his heart: never again will I curse the ground because of man, even though every inclination of his heart is evil from childhood. And never again will I destroy all living creatures as I have done' (Gen. 8:21).

All persons on earth were blessed as a result of Noah's sacrificial offering to the Lord. As long as the earth endures, seedtime and harvest, cold and heat, summer and winter, day and night will not cease.

God's response to Noah's sacrificial offering was in contrast to what God said in Genesis 6. God determined never again to destroy every living thing as He had done. Why this change on God's part? Was it because He realised that He had acted wrongly in blotting out the entire human race? Or was He frustrated over the fact that 'The imagination of man's heart is evil from his youth'?

The answer is no. The changed situation was bound up with the sweet aroma of Noah's sacrificial offering. Have you considered an offering that will provoke God to change His mind over your situation?

Abraham's Seed Offering and Tithing

Abram did not choose God, but God chose Abram to fulfil His promise in Genesis 3:15. Abraham responded with obedience to the invitation of God to become the father of a people through whom God would bless all the people of the earth. Abraham is a classic example of one who trusted God's leadership and served obediently according to God's commands. In a real sense, he was the second disciple after Noah.

Melchizedek means 'my king is righteous'. Melchizedek was the king of the city-state of Salem. He came out to greet Abram, bringing a present of bread and wine. This was the kind of gift presented to kings. When Jesse sent a present to King Saul, it included bread and wine (1 Sam. 16:20).

Abram responded in an acceptable and fitting way. He gave Melchizedek a tenth of all the goods he had captured from the enemy (Gen. 14:20).

Tithing began before the Old Testament tithe law was established. It was common among many religions. Abraham gave the first tithe recorded in the Scripture as a worshipful act of gratitude to God for help in battle.

Abraham Offered Care

The ancient Near Eastern custom of hospitality is clear here. It was an offence not to offer food and shelter to strangers at the door. Abraham offered hospitality to three strangers. Unknown to him, he was giving comfort to angels. 'Let a little water be brought, and then you may all wash your feet and rest under this tree. Let me get you something to eat, so you can be refreshed and then go on your way now that you have come to your servant' (Gen. 18:4–5). Abraham expressed the love of God in caring and hospitality, and got his blessing of the long-awaited covenant child.

Abraham Offered his Son

God tested Abraham's faith by commanding him to offer Isaac as a sacrifice to Him. In this case, God presented an opportunity for Abraham to clarify his loyalty. Did Abraham love Isaac more than God, or did he love God more than Isaac? Abraham passed the test and proved his absolute love for God.

This test is applicable to all believers. Do you love your life and your God-given wealth more than you love God?

Abraham's story is a remarkably moving account of faith. Nowhere else in the Bible does a man willingly offered to sacrifice his only son in obedience to God's demand, only to have God provides a substitute and a covenant of blessing and prosperity – except for the offering of the Son of God as a living sacrifice on the cross at Calvary.

The angel of the Lord called to Abraham from heaven a second time and said, I swear by myself, declares the Lord, that because you have done this and have not withheld your son, your only son, I will surely bless you and make your descendants as numerous as the seashore. Your descendants will take possession of the cities of their enemies, and through you offspring all nations on earth will be blessed, because you have obeyed me. (Gen. 22:15-18)

Three lessons are to be drawn from Abraham's willingness to offer his only son: (1) God does not require human sacrifice but does demand obedience and trust; (2) Abraham's obedience allowed God to bless him with intergenerational blessing and, through his descendants, bless all nations and generations of man on earth; and (3) the biblical principle is that we shall be blessed, but we are to bless in return and be a blessing to one another.

You can change the destiny of your generation with your seed offering and gifts like Abraham. 'By faith Abraham, even though he was past the age and Sarah herself was barren—was enabled to become a father because he considered him faithful who had made the promise. And so from this one man, and he as good as dead, came descendants as numerous as stars in the sky and as countless as the sand on the seashore' (Heb.11:11–12).

> Giving to the vulnerable, orphans, widows, victims of natural disasters, men and women of God, and the house of God is a necessity for believers and key to opening heaven for generational covenant blessings and prosperity.

Hannah was a woman who faithfully gave her long-awaited baby to the Lord in vow, even when the baby was yet to be conceived. Hannah's obedience to God revealed the depth and the genuineness of her worship. 'In bitterness of soul Hannah wept much and prayed to the Lord. And she made a vow, saying, "O Lord Almighty, if you will only look upon your servant's misery and remember me, and not forget your servant but give her a son, then I will give him to the Lord for all days of his life, and no razor will ever be used on his head' (1 Sam. 1:10–11).

Hannah relinquished the joy of her motherhood, the happiness of her broken barrenness, and the removal of her rebuke and shame from the surface of the earth. Hannah's prayer is one of the most effective prayers in the Bible. She began with an appeal to the almighty God. She prayed with earnestness, reverence, and humility. Her prayer for a son went beyond the Nazirite vow (Num. 6:1–21). She relinquished parental joy, happiness, and rights as an offering to the Lord.

King David also demonstrated the act of giving and sowing of seed offering by giving generously towards building the house of God.

With all my resources, I have provided for the temple of my God - gold for the gold works, silver for the silver works, bronze for the bronze, iron for the iron and wood for the wood, as well as onyx for the setting, turquoise stones of various colour and all kinds of stones and marbles, all of these in large quantities. Besides, in my devotion to the temple of my God, I now give my personal treasures of gold and silver for the temple: three thousand talents of gold and seven thousand talents of refined silver, for the overlaying of the walls of the buildings. For the gold work and the silver work, and for all the work to be done by the craftsmen. Now who is willing to consecrate himself today to the Lord? (1 Chron. 29:2–5)

Voluntary offerings are an indication of the heart which pleases God. Voluntary giving is a way of rejoicing in God and praising Him. It presents a sweet aroma to the Lord.

Then the leaders of families, the officers of the tribes of Israel, the commanders of thousand and commanders of hundreds, and the officials in charge of the king's work gave willingly. They gave toward the work on the temple of God five thousand talents and ten thousand darics of gold, ten thousand talents of silver, eighteen thousand talents of bronze and a hundred thousand talents of iron. (1 Chron. 29:7)

Blessing and prosperity are not ends in themselves, but the result of a life dedicated to service of God. It is clear that God wishes His children to prosper. How can someone dare to deny this? However, prosperity should not be an end in itself, but the result of a quality of life, devotion, dedication, and action that corresponds with the Word of God.

The words 'blessing and prosperity' literally mean to have success in every undertaking. They clearly imply that divine prosperity is not a momentary or passing phenomenon, but rather a continual and progressive state of good success and well-being. The phrase applies to all areas of our lives: spiritual, physical, emotional, and material.

God rejoices when His children prosper: that is, have blessing, prosperity, protection, happiness, and abundance. When our needs are satisfied, we have peace. Furthermore, if God rejoices in the prosperity of His servants, how much more will He rejoice in the prosperity of His children, those who were bought with the blood of Jesus and adopted as sons? Imagine how it will please God that we, His sons and daughters, prosper in all aspects of life.

Material Things Are to Be Used and not to Be Loved

God is not opposed to Christians owning material wealth. However, He is opposed to the material things possessing or dominating their lives (Mark 10:17–27). In Mark's telling, a young, rich man had kept the Law all of his life, but his riches dominated his life; he was not able to renounce material things, not even to the end of obtaining eternal life. There is no reason to doubt that if he had been prepared to dispense with those things, Jesus would have said that he could keep them.

This episode constitutes a sad example of what can happen when people put their trust in material goods, instead of entrusting all things into the hands of God who gave them.

It is a great responsibility to possess riches and wealth (1 Tim. 6:17). Paul tells us not to trust in the uncertainty of riches. We must not deposit our hope in riches, or expect that they will bring us security or freedom. Why would the apostle say that? Because riches are truly transitory and values change. Thus earthly riches represent only a passing value. An item that has value now could be worthless tomorrow. The wise thing to do is deposit our values, trust, and hope only in the hands of God, believing that He will make provision for us.

Even more so, we must never permit the possession of riches to make us think that we are better than others or give us the right to be irresponsible or negligent. It is a responsibility, a serious responsibility, to be the owner of a very great fortune. We must always remember that 'to whom much is given, much will be demanded' (Luke 12:48).

Do not trust riches. We must maintain our trust in God and allow our lives to be governed by His Word (Phil. 4:12–13). Let's permit these words to become a light that enables us comprehend God's will concerning the subject of blessing and prosperity.

The above biblical passage contains a yes (we may obtain wealth) and a no (don't trust in them). This perception demands our humility if we want to be blessed with riches. We are assured that if our lives seek the direction of the Word of God, then, through Christ, we may enjoy financial prosperity or temporary setbacks. We stand firm in our lives because our trust rests solely in the Lord.

If the economy falls apart tomorrow, God's people won't remain with their hands tied – that is, inactive, ineffective – because God is our provider, our assured aid. The Lord can protect us in times of need, just as in times of abundance. He fed Elijah, sending crows to bring him food in the morning and afternoon (1 Kgs 17:2–6). He can do the same thing now. God is the same today as He was before.

You're Prospered in Order to Be a Blessing

Abundance comes from God so that the believer can bless others. Deuteronomy 8 tells us that riches exist to verify the covenant, and shouldn't be squandered selfishly. Apparently, God wants our needs to be satisfied and wishes to suit the desires of our hearts. But once our needs and our hearts are satisfied, what should we do with the excess of His blessings? Can we live in more than one house at a time? God wants us to use our abundance to bless others.

God wants us to have wealth, but money is only a part of it. A person can have billions and still be poor in health, happiness, peace, friendship, and above all, personal relationship with God. Wealth is more than money and possessions. We need wisdom to receive the covenant of God's prosperity, to receive fortune without it controlling us, and to appreciate His achievement and purpose in our lives.

The blessing and prosperity promised by God in His covenant is always a means toward an end, and not an end in itself. God's plan is to enrich every human being. Jesus declares this wonderful intention to bless and prosper mankind in John 10:10.

God's covenant with mankind provides life in abundance. From the beginning of time itself, the Scriptures show us a God who wants our happiness and prosperity. In Genesis, God is revealed to us as He creates all things, declaring that they are good. Later, He gave this beautiful and abundant land to Adam, and granted him the authority to exercise dominion over all creation (Gen. 1:28). God's plan from the beginning was to bless and prosper all human beings. Jesus declares his intentions to recover and restore fully what the Father offered to man in the garden of Eden, and to destroy the Devil's attempt to hinder God's blessings from manifesting in our lives.

God does not promise anything without responsibility on our part. 'And all that he does will prosper' (Ps. 1:1–3). This includes everything: family, descendants, marriage, business, employment, health, and the work of the ministry. It signifies that God desires to fulfil what He says – everything will prosper.

No promise of God is exempt from some responsible action on our part. No one will prosper without doing what God says. Many people want the promised results without the responsibility or the obligation that accompanies it. That's wrong!

Every promise of God demands a responsible action on our part (Luke 12:15). Life is much more than obtaining and possessing material things. God wants us to enjoy a complete and balanced life. He made provisions through His Word so that we can enjoy the life that we receive from Him. The Lord has promised to supply our needs (Phil. 4:19) and has promised to satisfy the desires of our hearts (Ps. 37:4). But He also wants us to clearly define our priorities by 'seeking first the kingdom of God'. In this way, we must lean on and obey God first and 'all these things will be added unto you' (Matt. 6:33).

Do Everything the Lord Says and you Will Prosper

God is not stingy, but we have to do what His Word says in order to prosper. 'And my God will meet all your needs according to His glorious riches in Christ Jesus' (Phil. 4:19). This wonderful verse tells us that God will supply our needs clearly and conclusively, 'according to his riches in glory'. By declaring this, God makes it very clear that He is not stingy when talking about provision for His children. His riches embrace all creation, so there's nothing we need that He cannot provide. If we do what the Bible says, God will provide abundantly.

God promises to give all believers the blessings of Abraham and tells us that Jesus became a curse for us so that we may receive 'the blessings of Abraham'. This, of course, begins with our rebirth, becoming new creatures in Christ Jesus. But the 'blessings of Abraham' imply other things also. The Lord wishes us to prosper spiritually, emotionally, physically, and materially (Gal. 3:13, 14).

Wait patiently for your blessings and believe in His promises. 'But they that wait upon the Lord shall renew their strength; they shall mount up with wings as eagles; they shall run and not be weary; and they shall walk and not faint' (Isa. 40:31). This passage promises God's deliverance, strength, and blessings for all who are willing to wait according to His timetable. We must give our tithes and offerings liberally and joyfully, then watch and wait for the Lord to give back many times over what we gave.

Promises of Protection

From the days of Cain and Abel through to the days of Enoch and Noah and up to this present generation, the inclination of the hearts of men has been wicked. The Devil has possessed human hearts to perpetuate evil and to cause untold hardship, pain, war, and suffering.

Evil is not only the external, public actions of brutality that oppose the will of God, but also internal, secret, negative intentions and thoughts that destroy the peace of the world and all the blessings that were giving to humanity. Human morals will hardly improve and have not improved with passing generations. In fact, human depravity increased to the point where it became necessary for God to destroy all that He had perfectly created. Humans do not naturally choose to do good; we are more inclined to do evil.

The evil in human hearts continued to produce insecurity even after the flood. But in His grace, God decided to bear with man's evil ways rather than destroying all creation again. He promised protection for His obedient children and His elect.

The definitions of 'protection' are to safeguard, to defend, to provide safekeeping, to shield, to secure, to provide covering, and to care. This is the heritage we received from God when He promised to protect us. The Bible says, 'No weapon (evil) fashioned or forged against us will prevail and you will refute every tongue that accuses you. This is the heritage of the servants of the Lord and this is their vindication from me, declares the Lord' (Isa. 54:17).

This promise of God's protection is sure and certain. It cannot be broken. But it demands your commitment, faithfulness, and obedience to He who promised. Just as it is not possible for any sheep that wanders away from the presence of the shepherd to receive protection against the attack of the wild beast, so also it is not possible for any servant of God to enjoy the heritage of God's protection when they violate and disobey God's commandment. The Bible says, 'He who dwells in the shelter of the Most High will rest in the shadow of the Almighty. I will say of the Lord, He is my refuge and my fortress, my God, in whom I trust' (Ps. 91:1–2).

God has spoken very clearly and has given assurance of His protection to only those who dwell under the canopy of the Saviour. God is saying that those who rely on Him and obey His commandments need not fear evil.

God's primary responsibility to all His children and His elect is protection and security against evil aggression. Because of this, God has repeatedly told His children in the Bible not to be afraid. 'Moses answered the people, do not be afraid. Stand firm and you will see the deliverance the Lord will bring you today. The Egyptian you see today, you will never see again. The Lord will fight for you; you need only to be still' (Exod. 14:13–14).

Believe this truth, saints. The Devil and his cohorts will not stop their evil aggression against humanity in any form or shape, physically or spiritually. The Devil will attempt to use your relatives, friends, and colleagues to raise war against you, even from within your family circle. Sometimes the war can be a national war. Stand on His Word and promises of protection.

Never doubt His protection and deliverance, or disobey the Lord.

Let the cases of Jacob's sons against Joseph, Goliath and Saul against David, the nation of Babylon against Daniel, Shedrack, Meshack and Abednego encourage, guide, and strengthen your faith as you weather the storms of life. Let your faith dare every attack against you. Your God is watching over you to protect you.

The psalmist says, 'The Lord is my rock, my fortress and my deliverer; my God is my rock in whom I take refuge. I call on the Lord who is worthy of praise and I am saved from my enemies. He is my shield and the horn of my salvation' (Ps. 18:2–3).

As explained in chapter 1 of this book, however long it takes to obtain victory, protection by God is assured. In fact, the reason Jesus manifested on earth and came to die for you on the cross at Calvary was for your protection and victory. The Bible says, 'I am with you and will watch over you wherever you go and I will bring you back to this land. I will not leave you until I have done what I have promised you' (Gen. 28:15)

Promise of Victory

The ending of war, persecution, and affliction for the children of God is God's victory and a confirmation of the infallible word and sovereignty of God over every situation and circumstances. Paul and Silas were faced with national crisis as they were discharging their divine responsibilities; they were stripped naked, beaten, and thrown into prison. But God was with them and gave them unusual victory because they trusted in God whom they served. They cried to God in praise and worship, and He heard them and gave them victory. That is not common.

Abraham had victory over all his adversaries; so did Joseph, David, Daniel, Shedrack, Meshack, and Abednego. All believers have testimonies of victory one way or the other in their various life experiences.

Promises of Peace

Peace is the end result of victory over tribulations, wars, and afflictions. It is also the manifestation of the presence and sovereign power of God over every unpleasant circumstance in the lives of believers. Peace does not have its origin in this world but from God the Father, through His Son our Lord. The Holy Spirit is the agent of peace, a gift from God the Father through Jesus Christ, the Prince of Peace, who gives without adding sorrow, fear and pain. He expressly declares in the Bible, 'Peace I leave with you, my peace I give to you. I do not give to you as the world gives. Do not let your heart be troubled, and do not be afraid' (John 14:27).

Jesus promised peace for believers despite the activities of Satan and his cohorts on earth. Peace is not the absence of external conflict or hostilities. Peace is the power of internal security and assurance of victory of the cross through the death and resurrection of our Lord and Saviour, Jesus Christ. Peace is the result of deliverance from the power of sin and all its consequences.

Jesus sent the Holy Spirit, as promised by His Father, to bring comfort and peace into our lives. The issue of peace is the focus of God our Father for His children. The psalmist wrote, 'I will listen to what God the Lord will say; he promises peace to his people, the saints-but let them not return to folly' (Ps. 85:8).

Despite the assurance of peace by our Lord, there is a warning for believers not to return to folly. The Enemy of our souls could take advantage of our foolish acts to steal our peace. The psalmist described peace as a heritage for those who obey the precept of God: 'Great peace have they who love your law, and nothing can make them stumble' (Ps. 119:165). This clearly put the record straight: peace is conditional upon certain attitudes and behaviours. Since God is the source and facilitator of peace, He has a set of rules of life put in place in the Scripture that, when carefully followed, will automatically promote peace in our lives. Flagrant disobedience of this set of rules will automatically remove peace from our lives and give the Devil the legal ground to invade our lives and establish violence.

CHAPTER 6

Beyond the Natural

Salvation is the end result of all the promises of God – all prophecies as well as the earthly revelation of Jesus Christ our Lord, collectively with His finished work on the cross at Calvary (Heb. 1:1). Salvation is the expression of God's love for fallen man through Jesus Christ, in whom salvation was freely given and who ultimately restored man back to God (John 3:16; 17:21–22).

I have found no other way to explain the love of God for humanity other than the salvation He provided through Jesus Christ, His only begotten Son. Through Jesus, man was salvaged from the pit of hell into His marvellous light and glory. It is a confirmation that His love endures forever. From creation to salvation to eternity without end, God's love is sure.

Christ's death was the propitiation for our sins. His blood cleanses and erases all evil ordinances written against anyone who believes. His resurrection and ascension were the reason for the greatest name given to believers: that at the mention of Jesus Christ, every knee will bow down.

For is by the trespass of the one, death reigned through that one man; much shall they that receive the abundance of grace and of the gift of righteousness reign in life through the one, even Jesus Christ. (Rom. 5:17)

What an incredible transformation! Through a man called Adam, sin and death came into life. Through Jesus Christ, the Son of God, freedom, grace, and eternal life were restored.

So then as through one trespass the judgement came unto all men to condemnation; even so through one act of righteousness, the free gift came to all men to justification of life. (Rom. 5:18)

This is the reality of salvation: The Devil, sin, and death have no power where the Word, the name, and the blood of Jesus Christ reign, because Jesus had prevailed over Satan to open the seal of life.

And one of the elders saith unto me. Weep not, behold, the Lion of Judah, the root of David, that is of the tribe of Judah hath overcome to open the book and there seven seals. (Rev. 5:5)

And they overcame him because of the blood of the Lamb and because of the word of their testimony and they love not their life even unto death. (Rev. 12:11)

The truth of salvation is that only Jesus Christ, the Son of God, prevailed to overcome Satan and undo all the wicked ordinances of the Devil against man. No one in heaven or on earth was found worthy to do this great job except the Anointed One. The grace is the power of God that destroys the dominion of sin and death; grace also destroys the dominion of enemies, shatters their chariots, overthrows their horses and riders, and uproots the kingdom of darkness reigning over our lives.

The sweetness and the glory of the death and resurrection of our Lord Jesus Christ is grace. This informed our Lord's declaration, 'He who does what is sinful is of the devil, because the devil has been sinning from the beginning. The reason the Son of God appeared was to destroy the devil's works' (1 John 3:8).

The values of salvation are indescribable and incomprehensible. That God became man in order to die in place of sinners, so as to redeem man back to Himself, is truly marvellous. He took our sins upon Himself and gave us His righteousness to live forever. This is a divine exchange that is unbelievably amazing grace (Isa. 53:4–6).

> Amazing grace, how sweet the sound that saved a wretch like me! I once was lost but now am found, was blind but now I see.

Faith

Faith begins in the mind, from the moment a man believes that he is a living temple of the Most High God and a habitation of Jehovah Elohim. This is a platform in which man begins to function supernaturally, beyond the natural, and do all things through Christ Jesus, who lives and strengthens. This was the very platform where the apostles of Jesus Christ operated when they were translated from the realm of the law to the realm of grace.

Paul declares, 'Greater is He that is living in me than he that lives in the world' (1 John 4:4). Every one of Christ's generals, from biblical times to this present age, operated on this platform faithfully, to deal with and subdue every situation around them. 'I can do all things through Christ who strengthens me' (Phil. 4:4).

Jesus Christ desires this living faith from every believer. He wants them to live in the supernatural, to effectively dominate the natural things. 'Believe me when I say I am in the Father and the Father is in me or at least, believe on the evidence of the miracles' (John 14:11). Jesus Christ was simply saying that without the Father in Him and He in the Father, these miracles would not have been possible. He used this statement to teach on the subject of living faith, which requires all believers to faithfully trust God to be able to manifest the supernatural power in miracles, signs and wonders. He further commands believers, 'Remain in me and I will remain in you, no branch can bear fruit by itself; it must remain in the vine, neither can you bear fruit unless you remain in me' (John 15:4).

Friends, your living faith begins when you abide in God and God abides in you. Then you can begin to experience the miraculous power of God doing things for you beyond your natural strength.

This was the level at which David rose to challenge the bullying Goliath with 'five stones and a sling' in his bag. Declaring war against the boastful and bullying Philistine, he said, 'You come against me with sword and spear and javelin, but I come against you in the name of the Lord Almighty, the God of the armies of Israel whom you have defiled' (1 Sam. 17:45). David was not depending on his own ability to fight against Goliath, but faithfully depended on the God of Israel, whom the Philistine had defiled. God honoured his faith in the battle. David wrote, 'Some trust in chariots, some in horses, but we trust in the name of the Lord our God' (Ps. 20:7).

Remember, the strongest pillar that should hold your faith is 'God is dependable and trustworthy'. Hannah faithfully trusted God. Having lost her faith in man, she faithfully approached the throne of grace with a vow, placing a demand for God to do the miraculous concerning her barrenness. She demanded a boy who would be in the presence of God all the days of his life and she got what she asked for (1 Sam. 1:10–17).

Daniel, Shedrack, Meshack, and Abednego were also conscious of the presence of God in their lives. When they found themselves in Babylon as slaves, they resolved in faith never to defile themselves with food from the kitchen of the king (Dan. 1:8). The authorities of the land conspired against them and their God with a decree forbidding them from exercising their faith in the living God, only permitting worship of the gods of Babylon. They faithfully refused to compromise their faith and dared the gods of the land of Babylon (Dan. 3:8–30).

Get this message right, beloved. Once you allow God to dwell in you and you also in Him, God will surely honour Himself in you and contend with anyone, power or kingdom, who may be contending with you. This is the grace we're talking about.

The Babylonian authorities dared the living God in Daniel, Shedrack, Meshack, and Abednego. The Hebrews not only won the battle, but God also won the land of Babylon with a declaration by its kings that no one might worship other gods except the God of Shedrack, Meshack, and Abednego (Dan. 3:29).

Let me give further insight into a fundamental truth about the constitution of life to strengthen our faith. From the beginning of creation to eternity without end, the God who created the heaven and earth never gave legal right or jurisdictional authority to the devil to rule this earth. Devil was a defeated foe who was cast down to the earth (Rev. 12:7-9) he came to steal, to kill and to destroy. (John 10:10)

Human was created in the image and likeness of God, made kings and priests to rule this earth, not the devil. it is a great error and spiritual blindness for any man to be subjective to the Devil who is already defeated and now under our feet. Rev. 12:11 & Luke 10:18-19

Most great and successful men and women launched out in faith, gazing and projecting into the future with the picture of what they would like to become. They nurtured their faith in God until their dream manifested. Scripture says, 'Now faith is being sure of what we hope for and certain of what we do not see' (Heb. 1:1). Remember, you're created for dominion.

Faith involves absolute dependence on God. One's actions are based on certainty without any physical evidence. God is invisible, but faith is the human action which God counts as righteousness. Faith trusts God's promises even when they appear impossible. Faith reaches out to the eternal reward God has promised. Faith obeys God even when the divine demands appears unreasonable. Faith fears no human but God alone.

Faith perseveres and identifies with God's people even when no physical reward is in sight.

The faith of all Christians must establish its goal in Christ and His atoning works on the cross at Calvary. The list of faithful men in the book of Hebrews who received the reward for their faithfulness is living evidence to suggest to the present and coming generations that faith is powerful. Faith is the channel by which we can reach to the heart of God to please Him. Let there be a living faith in you to subdue every unwanted circumstances in your life.

Barack Obama, the first black man to become the American president, did not get there by accident. He got there through faith. He marched to the White House with the constant slogan, 'Yes, we can', and truly, he did.

As Jesus went on from there, two blind men followed him, calling out; 'Have mercy on us, son of David!' When he had gone indoors, the blind men came to him and he asked them: 'Do you believe that I am able to do this?' 'Yes Lord' they replied. Then he touched their eyes and said, 'According to your faith will it be done to you' and their sight was restored. Jesus warned them sternly, 'See that no one knows about this.' (Matt. 9:27–30)

Believe this truth, readers. Your faith is an important force that attracts the miraculous into your life, without which no one can please God. Your faith is required to defeat in every battle and overcome all enemies. What you believe is what you see; what you faithfully desire and confess in faith is what you get. Declare your faith ahead of you to finish the job for you. 'Then

Jesus said, "Did I not tell you that if you believed, you will see the glory of God?'" (John 11:40).

Faith is the spiritual horsepower directly connected to the throne of grace to bring miracles, signs, and wonders into physical manifestation. Faith is equally the main target of the Devil each time he afflicts. What he does first is to create fear and doubt in our hearts. This reduces our faith in God to zero level, so that we can deny our dependence on God and follow the Devil, and thence lose our heritage in Jesus Christ's eternal grace.

God is also testing and watching your faithfulness during your affliction to see if you qualify to receive the things of eternal glory and grace.

> Your faith is not proven until it has been tested as gold is tested with fire and you still maintain your faith in God.

Grace and the Tale of Two Trees

The scriptural account says that in the beginning, God created heaven and earth (Gen. 1:1). He planted a garden in the east of Eden. 'And the Lord God made all kinds of tree grows out of the ground – trees that were pleasing to the eyes and good for food. In the middle of the Garden were the Tree of Life and the tree of knowledge of good and evil (Gen. 2:8–9).

God created man to live a life of grace and to enjoy His abundant divine provisions with dominion – power to rule the fullness of the earth that was void of sin, suffering, struggling, pain, sickness, disease, and death. Under this dispensation, man was not meant to plant but to enjoy the divine provisions of God's grace. Human beings were to be in God's presence for worship and to dominate the earth on behalf of God.

This is the love and plan of God for the people He created in His image and likeness after His dialogue with His supreme heavenly council. Human beings continued to enjoy this wonderful grace until evil entered human history, when the Devil beguiled Adam and Eve to eat the forbidden fruit and lose grace.

Thanks to God, the messianic office was swiftly established for the offspring of the woman, who would be born with the responsibility of overcoming the Devil, redeeming and restoring humanity to the garden of grace (Gen. 3:15).

Before this unspeakable disaster, God had warned Adam against eating the forbidden fruit thus: 'You are free to eat from any tree in the Garden, but you must not eat from the tree of knowledge of good and evil, for when you eat of it you will surely die' (Gen. 2:17). This Tree of Life appears to represent the availability of eternal life for humanity in the garden, confirming that God's plans at the beginning was life not death.

However, God also created human beings with freedom or free will to sin and choose death, or to obey and choose life – hence the availability of the trees of life and knowledge of good and evil. God sternly warned man against eating the forbidden fruit and of the deadly consequences if Adam disobeyed.

The Devil clearly understood the grace of God for man and cleverly plotted to overthrow him and usurp the grace. The Devil devised a strategy of getting man to disobey God through

Eve. 'Did God really say, you must not eat from any tree in the Garden?' (Gen. 3:1).

The woman gave the correct answer but failed to understand the scheme of the serpent. She was completely ignorant of the plan of the Devil, who had come to steal, destroy, and kill. She mistakenly took him to be a friend with whom she could converse. The Devil took the chance to beguile Eve and cause havoc: 'You will not surely die' (Gen. 3:4b).

Regrettably, the woman fell into the deceitful plan of the serpent, ate the forbidden fruit, and gave the fruit to her husband, who also ate the fruit. Their eyes were opened. They instantly knew that they were naked, and their consciences picked at them. They hid away from God because sin had separated them from God. They had fallen from the grace (Gen. 3:6–8).

Now God had to call out, 'Adam, where are you?' The human beings had hidden and could not stand in the presence of God courageously, as they had done previously. Fear had gripped their hearts, causing separation between them and the throne of grace (v. 9).

The provision of salvation in the judgement of God for the Devil also provided the escape route for humanity against eternal damnation. God provided restoration of grace and eternal life, culminating in the series of covenants with Noah, Abraham, Isaac, and Jacob/Israel. The Law was given through Moses on Mount Horeb to prevent humanity from falling into sin again and to bring people closer to God for fellowship.

The establishment of the nation of Israel as a royal priesthood with a peculiar people is a typology of the church of Christ and the restoration of the lost garden of Eden, otherwise known as kingdom of God.

God progressively implemented His wonderful plan of salvation by using His elect, first among the Israelites and subsequently, upon the establishment of the church, among others raised to reveal His messages and promises of salvation. Amazingly, the Scriptures spoke without contrast about the coming Messiah, and finally manifested in the person of our Lord and Saviour, Jesus Christ, the Son of the living God.

The Bible says, 'For the law was given through Moses, grace and truth came from Jesus Christ' (John 1:17).

The law makes demands on man according to what God is. At most, the law remains a testimony of what God is (Exod. 25:21). But grace supplies human beings with what God is in order for humanity to meet God's demands. No one can truly partake of God's grace through the law but by His grace, which enables man to be in His presence to enjoy His abundant goodness, favour and truth.

The law compels us to struggle to meet God's demands and to work for God, but grace makes God meet our needs and work for us.

The Stories

The Tree of Life in the garden of Eden symbolised immortality. It was provided as a reminder that immortality is the reward for our obedience, while the tree of knowledge of good and evil symbolised mortality (Rom. 5:12–21).

	Tree of Knowledge of Good and Evil	**Tree of Life**
1	It represented the law, imputed sin into life, separated man from God and allowed death to show up.	It is a life-giving tree that enabled man to be in the presence of God, to enjoy His Grace, and to be like God.
2	It established the consciousness of good and evil in human mind, bringing with it guilt and judgement so that death could reign.	It compelled God to provide for the needs of man, as it was with Adam and Eve in the garden of Eden.
3	The law was given through Moses to bring man to the awareness of God and to judge human acts of good and evil.	It is the wisdom of God which creates the full awareness of God for perfect and sweet fellowship with God.
4	God cannot be pleased with the law. Neither can the law provide salvation; it only compels man to know and to obey God.	Grace overrides the law, sin, and death to give man unmerited blessings and eternal life.

The Tree of Life is mentioned ten times in Scripture. It is introduced in the garden of Eden along with the Tree of Knowledge of Good and Evil and is referred to in the book of Proverbs four times:

She is a tree of life to those who embrace her, those who lay hold of her will be blessed. (Prov. 3:18)

The fruit of the righteous is the tree of life, and he who wins souls is wise. (Prov.11:30)

Hope differed make the heart sick, but a longing fulfilled is a tree of life. (Prov.13:12)

The tongue that brings healing is a tree of life, but a deceitful tongue crushes the spirit. (Prov. 15:4)

Saints, the Tree of Life is a life-giving tree and very symbolic. It is a type of the Redeemer of the world who says, 'I am the way, the truth and the life, no one comes to my Father except through me." (John 14:6). Jesus Christ declared, 'I am the vine (tree) my Father is the gardener, (vine-dresser)' (John 15:1).

In this context, since God the Father, the Son, and the Holy Spirit are the source of eternal life and blessings, God expects man to make the Tree of Life the centre of his hope and life. Hence it is planted at the centre of the garden of the Lord, for man to continually draw from the well of grace.

Now, let's look at how symbolic and significant the Tree of Life is for the purpose of our understanding. The Bible says, 'In the beginning was the Word and the Word was with God and the Word was God. He was with God in the beginning; (John 1:1–2). This explains the prominent roles of the Word in the work of creation, revealing the Word as the creative power of God the Father.

The Bible states further, 'Through him all things were made; without him nothing was made that has been made. In him was Life, and that Life was the Light of men. The Light shines in the darkness but the darkness cannot comprehend it' (John 1:3–5).

Jesus Christ is the Word of revelation made alive in human flesh. His revelation did not begin at birth in Bethlehem; He has been actively revealing God since creation. He actively showed God's nature of Light and Life when darkness was over the deep of the earth and God spoke the Word and the Word brought light to subdue darkness and cause all things to live. 'In Him was Life', so the Tree of Life symbolises the Word revealed and manifested in flesh – Jesus Christ, the Son of the living God (John 1:14).

The account in the book of Proverbs says, 'She is a tree of life to those who embrace her; those who lay hold of her will be blessed' (3:18). Christ Jesus is surely the Tree of Life. He became the hope and eternal life for those who believes in Him (John 3:16). Proverbs also states, 'The fruit of the righteous is a tree of life and the one who is wise saves lives' (11:30).

You will agree with me that Jesus Christ is the Tree of Life, who became our righteousness through His living sacrifice on the tree of anguish and His death for sinners. He gave His body as flesh and His blood as wine for Holy Communion, to save and preserve our lives from mortality to immortality and for eternal life.

I absolutely love this scriptural record about the Tree of Life: 'He who has an ear, let him hear what the Spirit says to the Churches. To him who overcomes, I will give the right to eat from the tree of life, which is in the paradise of God' (Rev. 2:7). This verse clearly shows that we will once again eat from the Tree of Life displayed in the street in the kingdom of God. It signifies that everybody can freely eat from the Tree of Life and have it abundantly, as declared by our Lord Jesus Christ Himself: 'The thief comes only to steal and kill and destroy, I have come that they may have life and have it abundantly' (John 10:10).

The eschatological record in the book of Revelation also reveals the significance of the Tree of Life in the coming kingdom of God: 'Down the middle of the great street of the city. On each side of the river stood 'the tree of life' bearing twelve crops of fruit, yielding its fruit every month. And the leaves of the tree are for the healing of the nations' (Rev.22:2). The scriptural detail is synonymous with the record of Tree of Life in the midst of the garden, watered by river flowing from the midst of the garden, and suggests that the garden of Eden is the New Jerusalem in the new heaven and earth.

The grace of God carries the whole armour of God to do the miraculous in the lives of men, for the fulfilment of God's covenant promises. But you must trust and obey the Word and covenant promises of God. You are a candidate of God's grace. You are the beneficiary of the grace of God. He died for you and all humanity, to restore grace and truth. Let the grace of God be sufficient for you.

Point of Decision

Holy Communion is an act of divine exchange, climaxing with Christ's sacrificial propitiation on the cross at Calvary. Jesus Christ established and commanded Holy Communion as a divine ordinance, demonstrating His mandate given to believers. His sinless, incorruptible and righteous life takes away the human, sinful, corruptible, and destructible nature in exchange. He removes our inglorious life to give us His glory all unsought. Isn't that wonderful? What can be compared to this grace?

Jesus Christ said, 'I am the bread of life, your forefathers ate the manna in the desert and they died, but here is the bread that comes from heaven which man may eat and not die' (John 6:48–50). Jesus Christ thereby established a divine exchange in His command for Holy Communion, inviting every believer to the very point of decision of accepting divine exchange for our eternal life.

Jesus also used this divine exchange to establish a new covenant that will have its fulfilment in the kingdom of God. He declared, 'I tell you the truth, unless you eat the flesh of the Son of Man and drink His blood; you have no life in you. Whoever eats my flesh and drinks my blood has eternal life and I will raise him up at the last day. For my flesh is real food, and my blood is real drink. Whoever eats my flesh and drinks my blood remains in me, and I in him' (John 6:53–56).

The simple explanation to believers, for this ordinance of Holy Communion, is 'divine exchange', with which Jesus carried the assurance of resurrection and eternal life at the last day. Eternal life includes the furnishing of a body designed to house life at the last day.

Jesus made it clear that God is not an impersonal, uncaring God but a living God who is aware of everything that is going on around us. God is very much in control of the world He created and very active in the pursuit of salvation for the man

He created in His image and likeness. He is a living God who is the source of life.

Claiming the Promises

Whatever your situation, whether it is the loss of a job, loss of a loved one, going through a painful divorce, or being diagnosed with a life-threatening disease, do not lose faith! There is always light at the end of every tunnel, just as there is calm after the storms. God who delivered the Israelites out of slavery is the same God yesterday, today and forever. You can take comfort in knowing that He will neither forsake you nor leave you.

The Bible is full of God's promises; those are His words. Because His Word is true and gives life, we can use it to get out of any sticky situation. This lesson is about learning how to claim God's promises in the midst of the storms, pray God's words through a time of crisis, and come out victorious. This lesson is for anyone who is facing the storms of life, to help them rise above the storms in faith until victory is obtained through Christ Jesus.

It is one thing to know what God can do. It is another thing to faithfully claim God's promises even when all circumstances indicate impossibility. The extent of our faith is the anchor that provokes God to do unusual miracles, signs, and wonders through Jesus Christ. 'These signs will be with them that believes' (Mark 16:17). The pivot of our Christian life is to believe and trust that He can do it, followed by our waiting faithfully on Him in prayers and fasting, until His promises are made manifest in our lives.

Trust in the Word and Promises of God

Take a cue from the Word of God, which is the source of life and light. Everything else on earth has a dead end, but the Word of God lives forever. Claiming and appropriating the promised Word of God into our lives daily in prayer is the assured way to fulfilment of God's promises. 'Heaven and earth will pass away, but my word will not pass away' (Matt. 24:35). God will not fulfil His Word for the sake of any thing other than His Word, the Holy Spirit (the abiding God), and grace. Neither will He renege on His Word. Whatever He promises to do, He will surely do.

The Word of God is the creative power and architect of life, and the Holy Spirit quickens life. The Word was with God in the beginning, and the Word is God. All things were made by the Word (John 1:1–5). Claiming the promises of God demands without compromise that we abide in the Word, in prayers and character (John 15).

The Word of God and the Holy Spirit are the electricity grid that connects the earth with the throne of the grace of God to achieve the miraculous, beyond the imagination of man. It is the only assurance available to man, to claim our promises; there is no other way.

All other ways lead to destruction (John 14:6).

CHAPTER 7

The End Time

The entire human race was plunged into bondage moments after Adam and Eve ate the forbidden fruit. Sin and death were imputed into life, but with the act of righteousness by Jesus Christ, justification and life reign (Rom. 5:18).

My study of prophecy and signs of the end time as an ambassador of Jesus Christ afforded me the grace to understand God's prophetic agenda and redemptive road map for fallen man from Genesis 3:15 through to the restoration of man to His kingdom, otherwise known as new heaven and new earth (Rev. ch. 21 and 22).

Like Joseph, Moses was also a type of our Lord Jesus Christ sent to deliver the household of Jacob from Egyptian enslavement at the fullness of the four hundred years pronounced by God (Gen. 15:13).

Moses symbolises the coming Messiah, while the Israelites in bondage symbolise humans in bondage in the kingdom of darkness. The Bible says, 'He came to that which was his own but his own did not receive him. Yet to all who received him, to those who receive in His name, he gave the right (freedom) to become the children of God' (John 1:11–12).

The following are few similarity between Moses and Jesus Christ the Son of the living God.

Moses	Jesus
1. He was born when the Egyptians ruled over the Israelites as slaves (Exod. 18:19)	He was born when the Romans ruled over Israel (Luke 2:1–5)
2. Pharaoh ordered all Hebrew sons to be killed upon birth, but when his order was not carried out by the midwives, he ordered all Hebrew sons to be killed (Exod. 1:16–22)	King Herod ordered all Hebrew sons to be killed upon birth (Matt. 2:16)
3. When he was born, his mother hid him for a period of three months in Egypt (Exod. 2:2)	When he was born, he was hidden for an unspecified period of time in Egypt (Matt. 2:13)
Moses was initially rejected by His people and took a Gentile bride, Zipporah (Exod. 2:11–14)	Jesus was initially rejected and took the Gentile church as His bride (2 Cor. 11:2)
Moses was raised by a man (Pharaoh) not his natural father (Exod. 2:9–10)	Jesus was raised by a man (Joseph) not his natural father. (Luke 2:33)
Moses was sent by God to go and deliver his people to the Promised Land (Exod. 3:8)	Jesus was sent by God to deliver His people to His heavenly kingdom (Luke 4:18)

Moses used the blood of a lamb to protect the Israelites from death. The blood was also used to free the Israelites from bondage (Exod. 12)	Jesus was the Lamb of God who protected mankind from the bondage of sin and death with His blood (Heb. 9:11–15)

In the same way that Moses was sent to deliver the Israelites from Egypt to the Promised Land, so was Jesus Christ sent to deliver the world from the power of the kingdom of darkness.

King Nebuchadnezzar's Dream

The book of Daniel chapters 2, 7, and 9 are the most famous chapters in the Bible. God revealed His road map of redemption and restoration of His kingdom to Nebuchadnezzar, who ruled the world's most dominant empire, and to the prophet Daniel.

King Nebuchadnezzar had dreamt, and the dream troubled him. He woke up remembering that his dream had been disturbing, but he did not remember the dream specifically. The king called wizards, magicians, and astrologers and asked them to remind him what he had dreamed. Remember, he wasn't specifically asking for interpretation. He was simply asking them to remind him what the dream was.

The wizards and astrologers sought for time and asked the king to tell them what the dream was. The king was infuriated by their inability to reveal to him what was in his forgotten dream. He demanded that someone come forward to tell him the dream and its interpretation. No one could, so he ordered their execution.

Ultimately, it is Daniel who makes the dream and its interpretation known to the king.

The Dream

You, O King, were watching and behold, a great image! This great image, whose splendour was excellent, stood before you; and its form was awesome. This image's head was of fine gold, its chest and arms of silver, its belly and thighs of bronze. Its legs of iron, its feet partly of iron and partly of clay. You watched while a stone was cut without hands, which struck the image on its feet of iron and clay, and broke them in pieces. Then the iron, the clay, the bronze, the silver, and the gold were crushed together. And became like chaff from the summer threshing floors; the wind carried them away so that no traces of them was found. And the stone that struck the image became a great mountain and filled the whole earth. (Dan. 2:31–35)

King Nebuchadnezzar of Babylon was shown this dream so he would know what would happen in his kingdom after his death. At the same time, this dream was a revelation of the world empires that would be established after his, which include the everlasting kingdom of our Lord.

The fine gold of the dream image represents the powerful Babylonian empire ruled by Nebuchadnezzar himself (Dan. 2:38). The silver represents the Medo-Persian empire (Dan. 2:39). The bronze represents the Grecian empire. The iron represents the Roman empire (Daniel 2:40). The clay represents the future kingdoms that emerge from the old Roman empire (Dan. 2:42).

True to Daniel's prophecy, it was in the middle of Rome's long rule that God sent His only begotten Son to the world to set up the kingdom of heaven. The Christians, a small group of people that were drawn out of Judaism, have grown all over the world. Christianity became the Roman Empire's official religion under Emperor Constantine. The stone has truly grown to become mountain and filled the entire earth.

The church is a kingdom of God on earth that can never be destroyed but will stand forever and overcome all other kingdoms. Even the kingdom of Hades cannot prevail against the church.

The whole of creation is the product of the Word of God. From everlasting to everlasting, God is immutable, and His infallible Word prevails over every storms.

Prophecy and Signs of the End Time

Approximately twenty-seven per cent of the Bible was written as prophecy – a text equal in size to the entire New Testament! Bible prophecy is an enormously vital subject for those who desire to understand God's eternal navigation from the beginning till eternity without end.

Seventeen out of the thirty-nine Old Testament books are prophetic. All the books of major and minor prophets from Isaiah to Malachi are prophetic. Many of the psalms and Moses' books are prophetic. Most of the Gospels are prophetic. Some of apostles Paul's and Peter's writings are prophetic. The book of Revelation is prophetic. 'For no prophecy ever originated because some man willed it (to do so) it never came by human impulse- but as men spoke from God who were borne along (moved and impelled) by the Holy Spirit' (2 Pet. 1:21).

The Last Days and the Rock of Ages

The earthly manifestation of our Lord Jesus Christ in the midst of Roman Empire is prophesied in Daniel 2, including His ministry and the baptism of the Holy Spirit on the day of Pentecost.

As Jesus sat on the Mount of Olives, His disciples came to Him asking for Him to tell them when those things prophesied by Daniel would come to be. They also asked what the signs of Jesus's coming would be, and about the end of the age (Matt. 24:3).

Jesus replied and prophesied several signs of the end time that must precede the rapture, the great tribulation, His second coming, the destruction of old world, and the establishment of the eternal kingdom of God. These prophecies include:

- The appearance of false prophets (Matth 24:4–5, 11, 24)
- The occurrence of war and rumour of wars (Matt. 24:6–7)
- Multiple famines (Matt. 24:7)
- Frequent earthquakes. (Matt. 24:7)
- Apostasy from the faith (Matt. 24:10)
- Abating love (Matt. 24:12)
- Worldwide proclamation of the gospel (Matt. 24:14)

Some of these prophecies are from the time of Christ's manifestation, leading up to the time of rapture, the great tribulation, and the establishment of the eternal kingdom of God.

Jesus also made several prophecies to confirm those in the books of Isaiah, Jeremiah, Ezekiel, Daniel, and so on, including Matthew 24, Mark 13, Luke 21, and 2 Timothy 3 and 4.

Prophetically and precisely, the Bible is being fulfilled with amazing accuracy in these last days. This generation is seeing more of the Bible literally fulfilled than any previous generation that has ever existed in the entire history of mankind. 'Now when these things begin to happen, look up and lift up your heads, because your redemption draws near' (Luke 21:28).

We are living eyewitnesses to the prophetic Scriptures coming into rapid fulfilment. The unsaved around us are saying there is no God and asking questions about what is happening in the world. We the believers in this generation have a distinct advantage over all the previous generations, because the seal of Daniel 12:4 has been opened to us, so we can understand prophecy and signs of the end time.

For to us a child is born, to us a son is given and the government will be on His shoulder and he will be called Wonderful Counsellor, Mighty God, Everlasting Father, Prince of Peace. Of the increase of his government and peace, there will be no end (Isa. 9:6). The kingdom of the house of David in the Old Testament represents the messianic earthly kingdom of God. It gave birth to the hope for a heavenly messianic kingdom that will bring about the reign of God and the redemption of His people, as it was in the garden of Eden, known as the dispensation of the kingdom.

The Signs of the End Time

The following are signs of the end time, some of which were prophesy over 2500 years ago but now manifested in our present generation.

Increase in Knowledge and Travelling
'But thou O Daniel, shut up the words, and seal the book, even to the time of the end: many shall run to and fro, and knowledge shall be increased' (Dan. 12:4).

History had it that until very recently, within the last 150 years, the fastest means of travel was the horse. Today the world has witnessed the explosion of knowledge. Scientists are in the business of discovery and technological advancement. Now man can travel at hundreds or thousands of miles per hour. The mind-blowing fastest trains reach a top speed of 431 km/h or 268 mph. The biggest airplane, the A300-800 super jumbo, has a maximum economic seating capacity of 853 passengers.

Knowledge of the Word of God has also increased (Amos 8:12). Knowledge of the biblical truth was suppressed during the dark age of the church to focus on doctrines. But in these last days, God has raised the remnant of the church to take the full truth of the gospel, which was needed to fulfil end-time prophecy to the world before the end comes.

Rise of Deception, Occultism, and False Prophets
'And Jesus answered and said unto them; take heed that no man deceive you. Many shall come in My Name, saying, I am Christ ... and many false prophets shall arise and deceive many' (Matt. 24:4–5, 11).

We've certainly had evidence of this sign all over the world, with so many religious and occult groups increasing in different parts of the world. They are wolves in sheep clothing. To be a prophet, a person had to receive words directly from God's heavenly council. False prophets receive words from the satanic council of the kingdom of darkness to deceive the world. False prophets practice physical and spiritual adultery, apostasy, and syncretism in the name of religion. They raise false hopes based on their communication skills rather than on God's Word.

Satan often works through earthly political leaders and some religious leaders to implement His agenda on earth. God spoke against those false prophets in Jeremiah 23 and declared His wrath and judgement against those who deceive His people and encourage and strengthen wickedness and ungodliness. 'Then if anyone say to you, look, hear is the Christ or there' do not believe it. For false Christs and false prophets will arise and show great signs and wonders, so as to deceive, if possible even the elect' (Matt. 24:23–24).

The Bible forewarned against them and gave signs to identify them. False prophets have a form of godliness but deny its power, from such people, turn away. They parade themselves as men and women of God, speaking the Word but practising fetish and denying the cardinal doctrines of Jesus Christ. These doctrines are the Great Commission and the Golden Rule.

False prophets deny the reality of heaven and earth, the power in the blood of Jesus, the person of the Holy Spirit, the virgin birth of Jesus Christ, the second coming of Jesus Christ, and salvation by personal faith in Jesus Christ.

The apostle Paul wrote, 'The Spirit clearly says that in later times, some will abandon the faith and follow deceiving spirits and things taught by demons. Such teachings come through hypocritical liars, whose consciences have been seared as with a hot iron' (1 Tim. 4:1–2).

Paul is saying that in the last days before the second coming of our Lord, there will be falling away (apostasy, or mixing Christianity with paganism), with false prophets deceiving many, including believers.

Be watchful. Anyone who worships false prophets and the Antichrist will not have their names written in the Book of Life and will surely have their place in the lake of fire that is burning with sulphur.

Wars and Rumours of Wars
'And ye shall hear of wars, for nation shall rise against nations and kingdom against kingdom' (Matt. 24:6–7).

The above verses outline the increase in wars, terrorism, and unrest among the nations of the world. Records show that from the start of the First World War in 1914, which involved twenty-eight countries on six continents, to the conclusion of World War II in 1945, with virtually every nations of the world involved, over 100 hundred million people were killed, soldiers and civilians. Records also show that nuclear weapons, biological weapons, and chemical agents have been developed continuously since 1914. Current stockpiles of nuclear weapons are great enough to destroy the world twenty times over.

This generation is a living witness to the manifestation of this prophecy. Daily, world televisions carry news of wars. The hearts of human beings are failing to the extent that no prime minister, president, or national assembly can spent a week without talking about the threat of war.

Earthquakes and Natural Disasters

And there will be famines, pestilences and earthquakes in various places. (Matt. 24:7)

And there shall be signs in the sun and in the moon and in the stars and upon the earth distress of nations with perplexity, the sea and the waves roaring. Men's hearts failing them for fear and for looking after those things which are coming on the earth for the power of heaven shall be shaken. (Luke 21:25– 26)

This prediction of our Lord Jesus Christ over 2,015 years ago has become a reality in this generation. The world has witnessed several hundreds of earthquakes, tornados, and typhoons of high magnitudes that have killed several millions, destroyed properties, and wiped towns, villages, and livestock out of existence in several countries of the world. From 1990 to 2014, the following countries recorded large and deadly earthquakes: Japan, Indonesia, Chile, Afghanistan, India, Peru, Iran, Fiji Islands, Colombia, Costa Rica, China, Mexico, Haiti, USA, Taiwan, and the Philippines.

Definitely, this sign has been fulfilled in our generation more than any previous generation. We have seen seas roaring. Thousands have been wiped away by tsunamis, floods, and storms. The images have caused men's hearts to fail, particularly over the last fifteen years.

In these last days, the body of Christ must clearly recognise these signs and be motivated to hold forth for Christ before He comes.

Famine and Mass Hunger
'And there will be famines, pestilence and earthquake in various places' (Matt. 24:7b).

The famine that has struck the world over the last decades is unspeakable. Thousands are dying every day of starvation, and it is still spreading. Over one billion people go hungry in several regions of the world. Sadly, the amount of wasted food in the developed nations is more than enough to feed the starving population of the less fortunate regions of the world. Lands are becoming barren because of extreme weather called *climate change*.

'Therefore, shall the land mourn, and every one that dwelleth therein shall languish, with the beasts of the field, and with the fowls of heaven; yea, the fishes of the sea also shall be taken away' (Hos. 4:3). This prophecy in the book of Hosea did not only apply to the nation of Israel, but also to our present days. During the last few years, we have seen fishes, birds, and other animals dying in massive numbers. These are signs of the end time and fulfilment of the biblical prophecies.

Increase in Crime and Dishonesty
And because iniquities shall abound, the love of many shall wax cold. (Matt. 24:12)

But evil men and deceivers will go from bad to worse using deceit and being cheated on themselves. (2 Tim. 3:13)

This generation is a living witness to record high criminal activities and corruption like rape, drug dealing, stealing, and acts of terrorism. Teenagers' crimes are on the increase; police and government officials' corruption are at record highs in different nations of the world. This generation is witnessing full-blown sexual perversion: immorality, pornography, homosexuality, lesbianism and incest. Children are disrespectful to their parents.

Worse still, the people of the world today are entertained on television and radio and in magazines and cinemas by the sins that led the Son of God to climb the tree of anguish. We've heard of husbands killing their wives and children. We're also witnessing the era of suicide bombing in many regions of the world in the name of God.

Deadly Pestilence and Epidemics

'The earth dries up, and withers, the world languishes and withers, the exalted of the earth languish. The earth is defiled by its people; they have disobeyed the laws, violated the statutes and broken the everlasting covenant' (Isa. 24:4–6; see also Luke 21:11).

Pestilences are plagues and epidemics of deadly diseases, or pollution due to the dumping of toxic wastes into the air, water, land, and sea. These chemicals have polluted our environment to the extent that animals, birds, fishes, and other creatures are dying and plants are withering.

Pestilences include several insects that devour crops and cause discomfort, diseases, and death to millions of people.

Chemical pollution is threatening our lives at every level because the food we are eating is not as nutritionally rich as it was fifty years ago. This contributes to our health problems, especially cancer. Most assuredly, the Word of God concerning the signs of the end time has come into manifestation in this generation.

Breakdown in Marriage and Family
'But know this, that in the last days, perilous times will come: for men will be lovers of themselves, lovers of money, boasters, proud, blasphemers, disobedient to parents, unthankful. Unholy, unloving, unforgiving, slanderers, without self-control, brutal, despisers of good, Traitors, headstrong, haughty, lovers of pleasure rather than lovers of God' (2 Tim. 3:1–4).

Divorce has spiralled in many nations of the world, particularly in most Christian nations, in what appears to be a rejection of the ordinances of God. Single-parent families are on the increase and marriages are decreasing by the day. Many children are being abandoned and neglected by parents. Child sexual abuse or paedophilia is now a big scandal all over the world.

The world is presently going through perilous time with record high rates of divorce. Some sixty to seventy per cent of marriages end in divorce, especially in the civilised world. Child abuse is a major problem in most societies, and teenagers school are involved in smoking, drugs, alcoholism, and premarital sex. Girls seek abortions.

Pornographic magazines and videos, and television shows depicting homosexuality and lesbianism, are on the increase. 'If a man lies with a male as he lies with a woman, both of them have committed an abomination. They shall surely be put to death. Their blood shall be upon them' (Lev. 20:13). As a matter of fact, the world is saying no to God and disregarding the eternal law of God to say yes to humanism and Satanism in the areas of marriage, family, and relationships. Large percentages of prison inmates, school dropouts, criminals, drug abusers, and drug dealers, including prostitutes, are products of broken homes.

The world is also witnessing an epidemic of incurable diseases like AIDS that have caused the deaths of several million people due to reckless sexual immorality. The Word of God is true; we are truly going through a perilous time.

People Loving Pleasure more than God

'Traitor, heady, high-minded, lovers of pleasure more than lovers of God' (2 Tim. 3:4). This is true of our present age. We have stadiums of 120,000 seats filled to the brim while cathedral churches are empty or outright converted to residential buildings. We have seen pubs and amusement halls packed full while places of worship are abandoned.

Atheists and scientists have grossly advanced their campaign that there is no God, leading several million people in this generation to deny the existence of the supreme God.

An average person spends twenty hours a week watching television but finds it difficult to spend three hours a week to worship God. Television networks spend billions of dollars to cover sports like the Olympics, the Commonwealth Games, boxing, Wimbledon tennis, and other events worldwide.

Abominable forms of relationship are being introduced, indicating the rejection of the sovereign rules of God.

The Greek New Testament Bible says, 'They will betray their friends, they will be reckless and puffed up with pride, pleasure loving rather than worshipping God. They will put entertainment and pleasure in the place of God' (2 Tim. 3:4).

Signs of Space Activities

'And there will be signs in the sun, in the moon, and in the stars; and on the earth distress of nations, with perplexity, the sea and the waves roaring' (Luke 21:25).

This generation is the first generation to see men propelling themselves into space. We have witnessed the beginning of space exploration as prophesied by our Lord Jesus Christ. Please note that Jesus was teaching His disciples the study of astronomy, which is the pure science of studying the planets and heavenly bodies. He was not teaching astrology, which is an occult practice. As we all know, astrology is the practise of witchcraft and sorcery.

Today, mankind is preparing passenger spacecraft to travel to the moon and possibly live there. New planets are being discovered. Who can dispute your word, o Lord?

Men's Hearts Failing because of Fear
'Men's hearts [are] failing them for fear of the expectation of those things which are coming to the earth' (Luke 21:26).

In these last days, medical science has developed to its highest level in history. Heart disease has also reached its highest level. The strain of this terrible age is causing many people's hearts to fail. War and rumours of wars, earthquake, pestilence, and famine, in addition to incorrect diet, tension, stress, strain, anxiety, fear of the unknown, and extreme pressure all over the world have caused many hearts to fail.

In today's world, heart disease is becoming the number one killer all over the world because of the extreme pressure of the twenty-first century's lifestyle. The entire scenario shows that truly, God has the final say over His creation.

Distress among Nations without Solution
'And on the earth, distress of nations, with perplexity, the sea and the waves roaring' (Luke 21:25). Perplexity in this context means to be greatly embarrassed over a problem or problems that defy human solutions. Looking at current world affairs, the nations of the world seem helpless and confused over many issues like terrorism, economic problems, political turmoil, and the immigrant crisis, including civil wars in different nations. We are witnessing great crisis among the governments of the world.

Signs of Russia's Military Participation in the Middle East
This is a prophecy foreshadowed in the book of Ezekiel, chapters 38 and 39, with similarity to the book of Revelation, chapter 6.

Russia was drawn into the Middle East crisis militarily to support Egypt in the Suez Canal war in 1956, fulfilling the prophecy in Ezekiel 38:4.

Ezekiel 38 and 39 state seventeen times that Russia and her allies will make war against the tiny nation of Israel. This began with Russia's military involvement in the Suez Canal war in 1956, followed by Russia's supply of heavy military equipment to the Arabs to execute the Six Day War in 1967 and the Yom Kippur War in 1973. This certainly looks like an action replay of David and Goliath.

Many will argue that Russia was not in existence when God revealed the end-time war to be led by Russia against Israel. It is important for you to understand that the names of Persia, Ethiopia, Libya, Gomer, and Togarmar have changed with time. The Persian are now Iran; the Cush is now Ethiopia. Libya is Put. The Gomer, otherwise referred to as the Gimirrai or Gimmerians, were the ancestors of the Germanic tribe that fought and defeated the Roman Empire. That led to the populating of Western Europe. The French came from the German Frank tribe, and the English came from the German Anglo and Saxon tribes. Togarmah in this passage either refers to Turkey or modern-day Armenia, from which Russia came to be.

Israel is a tiny nation of royal priesthood, born out of God's covenant with Abraham, Isaac, and Jacob, confirmed to David and personified in Jesus Christ, the Son of God and the Messiah. Within the context of God's covenant with Abraham, God says, 'I will bless those who bless you and whoever curses you I will curse' (Gen. 12:3). This means that anyone or any nation that makes war with Israel is indeed cursing Israel, and God promised to curse that nation.

Thus says the Lord: Even the captives of the mighty shall be taken away, and the prey of the terrible shall be delivered: for I will contend with him that contendeth with thee, and I will save thy children. And I will feed them that oppress thee with their own flesh and they shall be drunk with their own blood as with sweet wine and all flesh shall know that I the Lord am thy Saviour and thy Redeemer, the Mighty One of Jacob. (Isa. 49:25–26)

God is the only One who has the key to lock, and no one else can open.

This generation has witnessed the era of the Cold War, in which two superpower nations, the United States and the USSR. contended to dominate each other. The United States supported and blessed Israel, and the USSR was involved in cursing Israel.

The Rise of Communist China
'And the sixth angel poured out his vial upon the great river Euphrates, and the water thereof was dried up that the way of the kings of the east might be prepared' (Rev. 16:12).

China. which came into world prominence when the communists took over governance, clearly fits into the prophetic declarations in Revelation 9 and 16.

China, which has been the most populous country on the planet, was weak because of backwardness, but now has tremendous military and economic capability. It is regarded as one of the four strongest nations in the world, and is in the fast lane to become the world superpower.

China's communist government officially declared in 1971 that China now has the military capability to field an army of 200 million men. This figure confirmed the prophecy in Revelation 9:16: 'And the numbers of the army of the horsemen were two hundred thousand, thousands. (200m) And I heard the number of them.' This figure has been confirmed.

The three frogs that came out of the mouth of the dragon, the beast, and the prophet are the demonic spirits that will work miracles to convince the kings of the east that they can fight against God and win. Certainly, there is no misunderstanding of their mission. They are coming to the battle of that great day of God to fight against God's army.

The nations will be gathered into the valley of Megiddo, which will be the battle of Armageddon. Jesus Himself will win the battle, and the kings who lent their power to the Antichrist will turn on him and destroy Babylon.

Middle East Peace Treaty
Therefore, son of man, prophesy and say unto Gog. Thus saith the Lord God; in that day when my people of Israel dwelleth safely, shall not know it? And thou shall come from thy place out of the north parts, thou, and many people with thee, all of them riding upon horses, a great company, and a mighty army: And thou shalt come up against my people of Israel, as a cloud to cover the land; it shall be in the latter days, and I will bring thee against my land, that the heathen may know me, when I shall be sanctified in thee, O Gog, before their eyes. (Ezek. 38:14–16)

People of God, the prophecies of Ezekiel in chapter 38 came into fulfilment in 1979, when Egypt made peace with Israel. The prophet clearly established that in the last days, when Israel dwells in safety in the land with her surrounding Arab neighbours – Egypt, Syria, Jordan, Lebanon and Saudi Arabia – Russia will invade Israel.

Russia will lose the great war. Ezekiel 38 says that when God defeats the coalition army that comes against Israel, He will do it with such force and such power that there will be a realization coming to many who were formerly doubting. God will be sanctified and made known among the nations of the world.

Sign of the European Common Market

In 1981, Greece became the tenth member nation of the European Common Market within the geographical boundary of the ancient Roman Empire, in accordance with the prophecy in Daniel 2. This ten-nation alliance has extended its membership to twenty-eight nations since.

Revelation 13:1 has similarity with the revelation in Daniel 2. Does this means that both the False Prophet and the Antichrist will emerge within the geographical territory of the Roman Empire? Let's wait and see.

Return of the Jews to their Primeval Fatherland

And I will bring again the captivity of my people of Israel and they shall build the waste cities and inhabit them, and they shall plant vineyard and drink the wine thereof; they shall also make gardens and eat the fruit of them. And I will plant them upon their land, and they shall no more be pulled up out of their land which I have given them saith the Lord thy God. (Hos. 9:14–15)

This is a great restoration of age spoken by God through the prophet Hosea to the Israelites, who were scattered all over the world.

The greatest problem of the Israelites was that they largely viewed God, who is the Creator of heaven and earth, as a localised god. Their misconception of Him was based on their disregard for the words of Moses and other prophets that God is God of all flesh, who created man in His image and likeness.

God in no uncertain terms let them know over 2,500 years ago that, no matter where they hide themselves or where they have gone, He will find them and bring them back to their land. God did what He promised to do when the nation of Israel was established in 1948.

Rebirth of Israel as a Nation
'And say unto them, Thus saith the Lord God; Behold, I will take the children of Israel from among the heathen whither they be gone, and will gather them on every side and bring them into their own land' (Ezek. 37:21).

Israel had been divided since the end of Solomon's reign as king over Israel. The north and south kingdoms had been invaded at various times, their citizens taken captive to different nations of the world. This prophecy says they would be returned to the land as one indivisible nation again.

This prophecy give us a clue to the Word of God which says that 'David my servant' will be their king, referring to Jesus

Christ, when God made an everlasting covenant of peace, and 'my tabernacle shall be with them' (Ezek. 37:26), referring to the new covenant that is in the blood of Christ (Luke 22:20).

God will bring them back to their land and will not leave them as flesh and bone. Rather, God will breathe His Spirit into them and they will live. Clearly this is prophesying that Israel will eventually receive the salvation of the Messiah. There is evidence of this in the present movement of messianic Jews.

I will plant Israel in their own land, never again to be uprooted from the land I have given them saith the Lord your God. (Amos 9:15)

Jesus made a profound prophecy on this rebirth of the nation of Israel symbolically:

Now learn this parable from the fig tree; when its branch has already become tender and puts forth leaves, you know that summer is near. So you also, when you see all these things, know that it is near, at the doors. Assuredly, I say to you, this generation will by no means pass away till all these things are fulfilled. (Matt. 24:32–34)

The fig tree stands for the restored nation of Israel, and this generation is the generation of people who will see the fig tree putting forth leaves from tender branches – that is, who witnessed the rebirth of the nation of Israel on 14 May 1948. Jesus used nature to convey a spiritual truth about the end time. Many mysteries of the power of God's Word have been demonstrated with the rebirth of the nation of Israel since 1948, and many more will be unfolded till eternity without end.

He will set up a banner for the nations, and will assemble the outcasts of Israel, and gather together the dispersed of Judah from the four corners of the earth. (Isa. 11:12)

I will be found by you, say the Lord. And I will bring you back from your captivity, I will gather you from all the nation and from all the places where I have driven you, says the Lord, and I will bring you to the place from which I caused you to be carried away captive. (Jer. 29:14)

Therefore say, 'Thus says the Lord God: "I will gather you from the peoples, assemble you from the countries where you have been scattered, and I will give you the land of Israel."' (Ezek. 11:17)

For I will take you from among the nations, gather you out of all countries, and bring you into your own land. (Ezek. 36:24)

Who is like You, o God? Your Word and covenant stand forever, but the fools says in their hearts, 'There is no God.'

Signs of Jerusalem Coming under Jewish Control
'And they shall fall by the edge of the sword, and shall be led away captive into all nations and Jerusalem shall be trodden down of the Gentiles, until the times of the Gentiles be fulfilled' (Luke 21:24).

This tragic prophecy of our Lord Jesus Christ concerning the future of the city of Jerusalem says that Jerusalem is to be conquered and controlled by Gentiles – foreign and unbelieving nations – until the time of the Gentiles is fulfilled.

Before the Six Day War of June 1967, Jerusalem had been under the Gentiles' dominion for over 2,500 years. Then the prophecy of our Lord Jesus Christ in Luke 21:24 was fulfilled. The newly established, tiny nation of Israel recaptured the ancient biblical city of Jerusalem. What a great, immutable God! His infallible Word can never fail.

The Monumental Outpouring of the Holy Spirit

And it shall come to pass afterward, that I will pour out my spirit upon all flesh; and your sons and your daughters shall prophesy, your old men shall dream dreams, your young men shall see visions' (Joel 2:28).

The Word of God is clear about this end-time Holy Spirit visitation and unprecedented revival (Joel 2:28– 29; Hos. 6:3; Zech. 10:1). The beginning of the fulfilment of this prophecy happened in Acts 2, when the Holy Spirit was poured out on believers in the upper room on the day of Pentecost. It continues to be fulfilled in our day.

The church of these last days is not destined for gloom or apostasy, but is destined to graduate from glory to glory to win millions of souls and nations through the supernatural gospel of truth.

Understand this truth.

The church that Jesus is coming back to marry to Himself as a husband is not the one that is being run over by the Devil. It is a glorious church that is running over the Devil through the uncompromising Word of God and the Holy Spirit, the abiding God with the name and the blood of Jesus Christ acting supernaturally.

James 5:7 indicates that the great harvest of the earth must await the 'early and latter rain'. Jesus says to His disciples, 'The harvest is great but the workers are few' (Luke 10:2). The Bible says, 'And another angel came out of the temple, crying with a loud voice to him that sat on the cloud. Thrust in thy sickle, and reap: for the time is come for thee to reap; for the harvest of the earth is ripe' (Rev. 14:15).

The ministry of the Word, teaching, and worship must be pursued vigorously in this end time.

Increasing Violence and Sexual Immorality
'Likewise also, as it was in the days of Lot; they did eat, they drank, they bought, they sold, they planted, they builded; But the same day that Lot went out of Sodom it rained fire and brimstone from heaven, and destroyed them all. Even thus shall it be in the day when the Son of man is revealed' (Luke 17:28–30)

Jesus warned the world concerning the coming days of tribulation, full of violence and sexual revolution, similar to the days of Noah and Lot in Sodom and Gomorrah. In Noah's day, the earth was filled with violence, wickedness, and ungodliness. In Lot's day, Sodom and Gomorrah had given themselves over to sexual perversion and immorality in which homosexuality prevailed.

In today's world, we are witnessing record high violence. Several nations have legalised same-sex marriage, and heads of nations are campaigning all over the world to introduce same-sex marriage against the sovereign rules of almighty God (Lev. 18:22–23). Watch it; it's the sign of the end time.

Persecution and Killing of Christians
'Then shall they deliver you up to be afflicted and shall kill you and ye shall be hated of all nations for my name's same. And then shall many be offended and shall betray one another and shall hate one another' (Matt. 24:9–10).

Because people hate the truth, they will not accept it. From the first century up to today, we have witnessed when religious bodies have ruled the world and killed tens of millions of God's people, a scenario that is now repeated in nation like Nigeria, Iraq, Iran, Libya, China, Pakistan, India, Egypt, and North Korea. Christians are being killed for their faith in Christ Jesus every day. This trend will also spread to the Western world once the mark of the beast is put in place.

Christians Turning away from the Truth
'For the time will come when they will not endure sound doctrine; but after their own lusts shall they heap to themselves teachers having itching ears; And they shall turn away their ears from the truth. And shall be turned unto fables' (2 Tim. 4:3–4).

This prophecy is also being fulfilled in this age. The majority of churchgoers do not study the Bible they're carrying but often quote what their pastors say. Others follow the wrong doctrine of their church elders or remain dogmatic according to Old Testament doctrines alone.

Jesus Christ described the Word of God as the truth that cannot be accept by the world (John 17:17). Paul warned of the task of teaching, because people would prefer teachers who fit into their views and teach only what their audience wanted to hear. Self-appointed teachers will deceive many with shallow teachings and expound the doctrines of men as if they were the doctrines of God (Col. 2:22).

Global Preaching of the Gospel
'And this Gospel of the Kingdom shall be preached in all the world for a witness unto all nations; and then shall the end come' (Matt. 24:14).

The true gospel must be preached to the world before the end will come. Has this prophecy been fulfilled now at this present age? Yes, it has. We have seen the gospel preached in different languages all over the world through radio, television, Internet, satellite, and magazine as never before. This last generation will hear the gospel before the end will come.

We are at the last days, when the everlasting gospel of Revelation 14 will be fulfilled. The 144,000 last-days evangelists redeemed with the blood of the Lamb from the tribe of Jews will join to carry the everlasting gospel of truth to the end of the earth. Then the end will come. Are you preparing?

Destruction of those who Destroy the Earth
'And the nations were angry, and thy wrath is come, and the time of the dead, that thy should be judged, and that thou shouldest give reward unto thy servants the prophets, and to the saints, and them that fear thy name, small and great; and shouldest destroy them which destroy the earth' (Rev. 11:18).

The pertinent questions are, are the nations angry today, and are men destroying the earth? Yes indeed, the nations are angry and men are destroying the earth. There are uprising and wars all over the world.

Contrary to the historical limitation of instruments of destruction to bow and arrow in previous generations, this generation has stockpiled destructive weapons of war. Due to chemical and oil exploration; the rivers and sea are completely polluted with dangerous chemicals every day from all over the world. Man is actually destroying the world more than ever before.

All of the human tragedy, suffering, and problems we are witnessing today are caused directly or indirectly by Satan and his human agents. None are caused by God. God still has a plan for this planet. Scripture has clearly outlined it within His Word. John 10:10 tells us of the destructive motives of Satan and the blessed and restorative purpose of our Lord Jesus Christ.

> 'None of all the Lord's promises he had made to the house of Israel failed, everyone was fulfilled' (Josh. 21:45).

The above twenty-five end-time signs are highlighted for the powers and principalities, the doubters and the atheists to know and understand that the earth belongs to God Almighty, the Creator. His Word prevails over creation.

God's Prophetic Timetable for the Future of the World

The prophetic timetable and events for the end time have been decreed and established by God, who created heaven and the earth. The mandate of the offspring of the woman in Genesis 3:15 cannot fail. Future events include the rapture, the great tribulation, the Anti-Christ, False Prophet, Christ Second Coming, the final judgement and the new age. I will highlight these events in this book but will delve more into these end-time subjects in my book *Thy Kingdom Come*.

Who are the Antichrist, the False Prophet, and the beast? What are their attributes and characteristic traits and scope of activities? We've heard about false prophets and the spirits of the Antichrist in the history of the Old Testament and the church age. However, there are the end-time Antichrist and False Prophet who will be revealed during the seven years' great tribulation after the rapture.

The study guide in the book of Daniel chapters 7 and 9 and Revelation chapters 13 and 16 clearly reveal the person of Antichrist and his activities that will have worldwide impact. The Bible prophecies teach both the Antichrist and the False Prophet will have their authority from Satan and operate with a high degree of evil.

The greatest works of the False Prophet are further revealed in Revelation 13. The False Prophet will disguise himself as a Christian, but he will not know Christ. His doctrine will be that of the beast, the Antichrist. He may not promote himself, so he will not become an object of worship. Rather, he will do the work of a prophet and direct attention from himself to the one who claims to have the right to be worshipped: the Antichrist. This will clearly reveal the alliance between religion and politics.

The False Prophet will duplicate many miracles of our Lord Jesus Christ. He will cause fire to come down from heaven, counterfeiting the miracles of Elijah. With this deception, the False Prophet will declare that since this miracle brings fire from heaven, it shows that the Antichrist is truly the Christ and should be worshipped (Rev. 13:13–14).

He will appear as a Christian, even though his doctrine is anti-Christian. Be watchful. We've heard about how the extremist religionist kills Christians for preaching Christianity. They easily convert and convince people to kill in the name of religion and their gods.

Worship cannot be forced. One can be forced to bow down but cannot be forced to worship. Anyone who worships the False Prophet and the Antichrist will surely not have their names written in the Book of Life of our Lord Jesus Christ.

The Rapture

And if I go and prepare a place for you, I will come again and receive you to myself; that where I am, there you may be also. (John 14:3)

Behold, I tell you a misery: we shall not all sleep, but we shall all be changed. In a moment, in a twinkling of an eye, at the last trumpet, for the trumpet will sound, and the dead will be raised incorruptible, and we shall be changed. For the corruptible must put on incorruptible, and this mortal must put on immortality. (1 Cor. 15:51–53)

For the Lord Himself will descend from heaven with a shout, with the voice of an archangel, and with the trumpet of God.

And the dead in Christ will rise first, Then we who are alive shall be caught up together with them in the clouds to meet the

Lord in the air. And thus we shall always be with the Lord. (1 Thess. 4:16–17)

The rapture is the next great event in God's prophetic calendar, and it may occur any time. It will be a miraculous event when Jesus Christ will appear in midair, the dead will rise first from the grave, and the righteous living members of the church (the saints) shall be transformed to be with Him to receive resurrected bodies. This event will be followed with the seven years' great tribulation period.

The word 'rapture' is not found in the Bible. It means 'ecstatic joy or snatching away or catch up'. It will be a period of unparalleled joy for the church of Jesus Christ. the rapture is a distinct supernatural event different from Christ's second coming.

Christians are the ambassadors of Jesus Christ, and the church is the kingdom of God's embassy on earth. Whenever a nation wants to declare war against another nation, that nation will first recall her ambassador. Such an event is the rapture. Jesus, who is the King of the kingdom of God, will appear in the sky to recall His own out of the world before He begins to pour out His wrath on this wicked world. It will be similar to the calling of Lot from Sodom by God before He poured out fire and brimstone on the city.

The rapture is a different supernatural event from the second coming of our Lord Jesus Christ. These separate events must be thoroughly explained, studied, and understood by all. Hence the scriptural saying, 'Be always on the watch, and pray that you may be able to escape all that is about to happen, and that you may be able to stand before the Son of Man' (Luke 21:36).

Contrast between the Rapture and Christ's Second Coming

Rapture	Christ's Second Coming
1. It occurs before the great tribulation (Luke 21:36)	It occurs after the great tribulation (Matt. 24:29–30)
2. Christ comes for the saints (1 Thess. 4:13–17)	Christ comes with the saints (Jude 14; Rev. 19:11–21)
3. Christ takes the saints to heaven (John 14:3)	Christ brings the saints back to earth (Zech. 14:4–5; Rev. 19:14)
4. Christ returns to the clouds (1 Thess. 4:17)	Christ returns to the earth (Zech. 14:4–5)
5. Christ is not seen (1 Cor. 15:52)	Every eye shall see Christ (Rev. 1:7)
6. It is the blessed hope of the saints (Titus 2:13)	It is the great days of His judgement (Rev. 19:15)
7. Christ does not come to destroy the Antichrist at the rapture, but to remove the saints so that the Antichrist can be revealed (2 Thess. 2:1–8)	Christ comes back to the earth with all the saints of all the ages at His second coming to destroy the Antichrist and his forces (Rev. 19:11–21)
8. There will be no battle of Armageddon at the rapture (1 Thess. 4:16)	The battle of Armageddon will be fought at His second coming (Zech. 14)
9. No man will know who the Antichrist is at the time of the rapture (2 Thess. 2:7–8)	All men on earth will know who the Antichrist is at Christ's second coming (Rev. 13:16–18)

10. There will be a seven-year period of tribulation after the rapture (Dan. 9:27)	There will be no tribulation at all when He shall come. All suffering will end.
11. The rapture is a mystery that was not revealed in the Old Testament.	The second coming of our Lord was revealed in both Old and New Testaments.
12. The saints will be rewarded in heaven after the rapture at the judgement seat of Christ according to their works.	After Christ's second coming, He will judge the living nations on the earth.

The world had witnessed three scriptural records of previous raptures of individuals in the Bible.

- The rapture of Enoch in Genesis 5:21–24 almost 5,180 years ago, which was also confirmed in Hebrews 11:5.
- The rapture of Elijah over 3,500 years ago, when he was taken up bodily into heaven in 2 Kings 2:1, 8–12.
- The rapture of our Lord Jesus Christ after His resurrection, when He went up to heaven in His physical body at His ascension (Acts 1:9–11).

The fourth rapture will involve all the living saints and the dead in Christ, according to the scriptural record (Matt. 25:36–41). *Be prepared.*

The Great Tribulation

This is a period of seven years on earth after the rapture of the saints, as prophesied in the books of Daniel, Matthew, and Revelation. The great tribulation will witness unequalled satanic activities on earth, with wickedness, war, and higher rates of destruction and disturbance. It will be a very difficult period for Israel as well.

We call this period the great tribulation because it will be the worst time of trouble earth has ever had, according to biblical prophecy (Dan. 9:27; Matt. 24:15–31; Isa. 66:7–8; Rev. 7:14; 19:21).

This is the period prophesied in 2 Thessalonians 2 and Revelation 6, when the Antichrist will be revealed. Although we know that the spirit of the Antichrist is alive today, even from before the inception of the church, and active in the political arena to obscure the truth and change the law of God, the Antichrist called the son of perdition will not be revealed until after the rapture.

The Antichrist

The Antichrist is Satan's agent. He will begin his seven-year satanic assignment only at the beginning of the great tribulation. He will deceive Israel into a peace agreement, which he will renege upon in the middle of the seven years (Dan. 9:27). The 'he' in Daniel 9:27 is the 'prince that shall come' in verse 26, the Antichrist who will deceive Israel. He will not be revealed to the world until after the ten kingdoms in Daniel 7:23–24 are formed within the boundaries of the old Roman Empire, and until after the rapture of the saints as prophesied in 2 Thessalonians 2:6–8. He will operate within the last week of Daniel's seventy weeks between the rapture, known at the great Tribulation and the second coming of Christ.

And the ten horns out of this kingdom are ten kings that shall arise and another shall rise after them; and he shall be diverse from the first and he shall subdue three kings. And he shall speak great words against the most High, and shall wear out the saints of the most High and think to change times and laws and they shall be given unto his hand until a time and times and the dividing of time. (Dan. 7:24–25; 17:12–13).

This refers to the Antichrist, who will rise to great power following the rapture. He will attempt to control and conquer the world, and will strongly oppose Jesus Christ and the programme of God for humanity. He will attempt to change the law in the last days.

The Antichrist will not be a worldwide dictator; neither will he be president of one world government, since the government of this world is on the shoulders of Jesus, the Son of God (Isa. 9:6).

The Antichrist will be a liar, deceiver, boaster, and homosexual; he will persecute the saints who believe in Jesus Christ, and will rise up against Israel with his alliance armies. He will be defeated by the strong army of Jesus Christ from heaven, and he will be cast into the lake of fire (Dan. 7:26–27; Rev. 17:14).

Mark of the Beast

At the beginning of the second half of the seven-year tribulation period, the Antichrist who previously set himself up as a man of peace will suddenly move against Israel. The Antichrist will cause all – small and great, rich and poor, free and slave – to receive a mark on their right hand or on their foreheads. No one may buy or sell except one who has the mark or the name of the beast or the number of his name (666) (Rev. 13:16– 17).

The world is trying to make cash obsolete and is actively pushing for electronic forms of payment by introducing Google Wallet, PayPal, and the electronic banking debit and credit card system.

For instance, Nigeria is currently deploying biometric technology throughout her banking system. Sweden is close to cashless society. Israel's government is advocating a cashless system. The UN world food program is pushing for a smart card and digital payment system.

This technology is not, on its own, the mark of the beast, but it lays the groundwork needed to implement the mark of the beast. It will help to establish a unified system that will make it possible to introduce the mark of the beast. This present generation is a living witness to the fulfilment of the signs of the end time.

The Second Coming of Christ

And in the days of these kings, the God of heaven will set up a kingdom which shall never be destroyed; and the kingdom shall not be left to other people: it shall break in pieces and consume all these kingdoms, and it shall stand forever. Inasmuch as you saw that the stone was cut out of the mountain without hands, and that it broke in pieces the iron, the bronze, the clay, the silver, and the gold. The great God has made known to the king what will come to pass after this. The dream is certain, and the interpretation is sure. (Dan. 2:44–45)

At the end of the seven years' tribulation period, Jesus Christ will physically return to the earth with His angels and those believers who were previously raptured (Matt. 23 and Rev. 19).

First, He will destroy the Antichrist and his army in the battle of Armageddon, and establish His everlasting kingdom that cannot be destroyed. When Christ comes, His arrival will not be secret. It will be like a bolt of lightning that will illuminate the whole earth in a magnificent way (Matt. 24:27). He will come exactly as He ascended and departed from the earth (Acts 1:9) to seat at the right hand of God the Father (Acts 1:10– 11).

At His second coming, Christ will step on the Mount of Olives (Acts 1:12; Zech. 14:4). His return will cause an earthquake that will split the Mount of Olives and open up a very large valley, half to the north and half to the south (Zech. 14:4).

The Bible describes the appearance of His descent with the armies of heaven as being like a Roman general riding on a white stallion, our triumphant King of Kings and Lord of Lords.

And in that day, His feet will stand on the Mount of Olives, which faces Jerusalem on the east. And the Mount of Olives shall be split in two, from east to west,. Making a very large valley; half of the mountain shall move toward the north and half of it toward the south. (Zech. 14:4)

Christ's second coming will be in the full view of the people of the world.

I was watching in the night visions, and behold, One like the Son of Man, coming with the clouds of heaven! He comes to the Ancient of Days, and they brought Him near before Him.

Then to Him was given dominion and glory and a kingdom that all the peoples, nations and languages should serve Him. His dominion is everlasting dominion, which shall not pass away, and His kingdom the one which shall not be destroyed. (Dan. 7:13–14)

Jesus Christ spoke about His second coming in the following parables:

- Parable of the fig tree (Matt. 24:32–33)
- Parable of the good man of the house (Matt. 24:43–44)
- Parable of the faithful servant (Matt. 24:45– 51)
- Parable of the ten virgins (Matt. 25:1–13)
- Parable of the talents (Matt. 25:14–30)

How glorious and beautiful it is that the book of Revelation draws the inspired Book of Life to a conclusion with three timely promises of the second coming of our Lord. Those who are preparing themselves to witness the second coming of our Lord and following the revelation of God in the Bible are fortunate.

Jesus declared, 'Behold, I am coming soon! Blessed is he who keeps the words of the prophesy in this book' (Rev. 22:7, 12, 20). Christ will appear again, this time not as the Lamb, but as the King of Kings and Lord of Lords, to restore the perfection of all things as it was in the beginning. The sense of urgency in this promise, in contrast to Christ's delay, leaves believers with the awareness that the Lord of life simply wants His redeemed children to be alert at all times.

The return of Christ from heaven with clouds will be a reversal of the manner of His departure (Acts. 1:9). His coming will have a universal impact; every eye will see Him. 'Look, he is coming with the clouds, and every eye will see him, even those who pierced him; and all the people of the earth will mourn because of him. So shall it be! Amen. "I am the Alpha and the Omega," says the Lord God, "who is, and who was, and who is to come, the Almighty"' (Rev. 1:7–8). Christ will return visibly and in great glory for all to see.

Jesus declared, 'Behold, I am coming soon! My reward is with me, and I will give to everyone according to what he has done. I am the alpha and the Omega, the First and the Last, the Beginning and the End' (Rev. 22:12).

The pertinent question in mind should be, what sort of reward is Jesus coming to give, apart from eternal life? There are five crown rewards for our faithfulness in Him.

The Crown of Righteousness

This crown is for those believers who were ready and waiting for the return of Jesus – all those who have longed for His appearing. 'Finally, there is laid up for me the CROWN OF RIGHTEOUSNESS which the Lord the righteous judge will give to me on that Day and not to me only but also to all who have loved His appearing' (2 Tim. 4:8).

The Incorruptible Crown

This is the victor's crown for those who disciplined their bodies, brought them into subjection, and had self-control.

Everyone who competes in the games goes into strict training. They do it to get a crown that will not last; but we do it to get a crown that will last forever. Therefore I do not run like a man running aimlessly, I do not fight like a man beating for the air.

No, I beat my body and make it my slave so that after I have preached to others, I myself will not be disqualified for the prize. (1 Cor. 9:25–27)

The Crown of Life

This is the martyr's crown for those who are faithful unto death, those who patiently endure testing, temptations, and trials.

Blessed is the man who perseveres under trial, because when he has stood the test, he will receive the crown of life that God has promised to those who love him. (Jas. 1:12)

Do not be afraid of what you are about to suffer. I tell you, the devil will put some of you in prison to test you, and you will suffer persecution for ten days. Be faithful even to the point of death and I will give you the crown of life. (Rev. 2:10)

Do your best to present yourself to God as one approved, a workman who does not need to be ashamed and who correctly handles the word of truth. (2 Tim. 2:15)

The Crown of Glory

This is the elder's crown. This crown is for those leaders – apostles, prophets, evangelists, pastors, teachers, deacons, deaconesses and elders – who were a godly example to the flock of believers that was entrusted to their care. 'Care for the FLOCK God has entrusted to you watch over it willingly, not for what you will get out of it, but because you are eager to serve God. DON'T LORD IT OVER THE PEOPLE ASSIGNED TO YOUR CARE, but LEAD them by your own GOOD EXAMPLE. And when the Chief Shepherd appears, you will receive the CROWN OF GLORY that does not fade away' (1 Pet. 5:2–4).

The Crown of Rejoicing

This is the soul winner's crown, for believers who are obeying Jesus's Great Commission (Matt. 28:19–20).

For what is our hope, or joy, or CROWN OF REJOICING? Is it not even YOU in the presence of our Lord Jesus Christ at His coming? (1 Thess. 2:19)

Those who are wise will shine as bright as the sky, and those who LEAD MANY TO RIGHTEOUSNESS will shine like stars forever. (Dan. 12:3)

The Crown of Gold

The above scriptural facts about the second coming of our Lord Jesus Christ reveal that Jesus's mandate is not limited to restoring eternal life and making ways for believers' entrance into the kingdom of God. He is also coming to reward believers for our faithfulness to His commands. Our love towards one another, our diligence to the service of the Lord, and our truthfulness to one another and to the Lord attract various crown rewards. But the greatest of all the awards is the grace for believers to sit with Him in His Glory, to judge the angels, and to reign with Him forever and ever in His Glorious kingdom.

Then I saw heaven opened, and behold, a white horse. And he who sat on Him was called Faithful and True, and in righteousness He judges and makes war. His eyes were like a flame of fire, and on is head were many crowns, He had a name written that no one knew except Himself. He was clothed with a robe dipped in blood, and his name is called the Word of God. And the armies in heaven, clothed in fine linen, white and clean, followed Him on white horses. Now out of His mouth goes a sharp sword, that with it He should strike the nations. And he Himself will rule them with a rod of iron. He Himself treads the winepress of the fierceness and wrath of Almighty God. And he has on His robe and on His thigh a name written: KING of kings, LORD of lords. (Rev. 19:11–16)

Disparities between His First and Second Coming

Christ's first manifestation	Christ second coming
He came as a Saviour	He will come as a King to reign
He came as Lamb of God	He will come as the Lion of the tribe of Judah
He came to wear the crown of thorns	He will come to wear the royal diadem
He came to die in anguish on the cross	He will come to reign on a glorious throne
He rode on the foal of an ass as the man of Galilee	As a King of Kings, He will ride a white stallion

He came as a white servant in humility	Christ will come as a judge in power
He was beaten with the rods	He will rule the nations with a rod of iron
He was rejected by His own	Every knee shall bend and every tongue shall confess that Jesus Christ is the Lord to the glory of God the Father

Behold, I come quickly: blessed is he that keepeth the sayings of the prophecy of this book (Rev. 22:7).

The Final Battle of the Lord

This war will occur at the end of the seven-year tribulation period, when our Lord Jesus Christ will come down with the armies of heaven and wipe out the combined armies of the Antichrist plus the 200 million strong Oriental army. The bloodbath will flow for over two hundred miles in the valley of Megiddo in Israel (Rev. 14:20; 19:11–21).

This will be the final battle gathered by the Antichrist against the Lord. The Antichrist will be thoroughly defeated. Christ's final victory will bring to an end this evil world to establish the kingdom of God and His rule over all creation. 'The seventh angel sounded his trumpet and there were loud voices in heaven which said: The kingdom of the world has become the kingdom of our Lord and of his Christ and he will reign for ever and ever' (Rev. 11:15).

All worldly evil is for an appointed time, but God's sovereign authority and power are eternal.

Eternal Life and the Kingdom of God

The vision of the new age to come is told in terms of a new heaven and a new earth. Newness is the sum expression of the kingdom of God, where the sovereign God reigns with the redeemed who will see and know God face-to-face in His glory. This was only made possible with the victory of our Lord Jesus Christ on the cross.

The kingdom of God, otherwise known as a new heaven and a new earth, is where the Son of God rules as the King of Kings and Lord of Lords. Eternal life is the very life of God that was lost in the garden of Eden, in a new arena of existence of life without end. The kingdom of God and eternal life are the end result of the promised offspring of the woman (Genesis 3:15). The death, resurrection, and ascension of the Son of God, our Lord, is the very essence of the sacrificial gift of the Begotten Son by the Father. It is the very reason for the manifestation of the Son of God to destroy the works of darkness and to restore the lost garden of Eden, called New Jerusalem (Rev. 21:1–7). It is the reason for Christ's second coming.

God originally created the earth to be an everlasting home for humans, but sin entered and changed the earth into a place of disobedience, rebellion, and alienation from God. The Bible tells how God has been working throughout history to effect a total reversal of this terrible consequence brought to life by sin.

Through the first coming of Jesus Christ, the Lamb of God, sin was defeated. The second coming of Christ will reveal the new kingdom of God. All suffering will be eliminated (Rev. 7:16). The limitations and problems of this age will disappear. The negative history of this earth will end in the new life. Death will be swallowed in victory, and the Devil will be thrown into the lake of fire, burning with sulphur along with his angels forever (Rev. 19:17–21; 20:1–10).

In this order, the age-long Adversary of humanity was an embryo in Genesis 3:15 and reaffirmed by Jesus in Revelation 12:11. The Devil was in principle defeated on the cross at Calvary (Heb. 2:14). The preliminary manifestation of his defeat was his binding for a thousand years in the pit (Rev. 20:1–3). The establishment of the eternal kingdom of God will be preceded by the eternal confinement of Satan and his angels in the lake of fire (Rev. 19:17–21; 20:7–10).

In the new heaven and earth, God promises to be with man as the Father of a united family. All humanity will be in His Presence, and He will wipe off all tears and sorrow and eliminate persecutions, suffering, sicknesses, diseases, and death completely. Our sovereign God will be the absolute and supreme Governor-General over eternal life, where worship, peace, and joy reign.

Revelation chapters 21 and 22 reveal the life, structures, and glory of the coming kingdom of God. Gold, the most valuable natural resources here on earth, will be the least valuable in the kingdom of God. Some major and minor prophets foretold concerning the kingdom of God. Jesus Christ, the Son of the living God, repeatedly taught about the kingdom of God at every opportunity available.

The wicked and the ungodly will not be allowed to enter this golden and everlasting age. Let's take a stroll into the kingdom where the glory of God reigns without suffering, as graphically revealed to John:

And he carried me away in the Spirit to a mountain great and high, and showed me the great city Jerusalem, coming down out of heaven from God. It shone with the Glory of God and its brilliance was like that of a very precious jewel, like jasper, clear as crystal. It had a great high wall with twelve gates and with twelve angels at the gate. On the gate were written the names of the twelve tribes of Israel. There were three gates on the east, three on the north, three on the south and three on the west. The wall of the city had twelve foundations, and on each of them were the names of the twelve apostles of the Lamb. (Rev. 21:10–14)

Here, the King of life took His anointed messenger in His Spirit and showed him the future of life that has been designed and made perfect by God, working perfectly, without evil and imperfection, as He intended life to be.

The glory of God is the shining radiance and the expression of what God is. 'The city does not need the sun or the moon to shine on it, for the glory of God gives it light, and the Lamb is its Lamp' (v. 23). God will be fully disclosed to His children, who will see and know Him in the full radiance of His glory.

This is the ultimate result of the sacrifice of the Lamb of God on the cross at Calvary. The wicked and the ungodly will never be allowed to enter this golden and everlasting age (v. 27).

The glory of God's kingdom, as explained in the book of Revelation, is unspeakable; the least in value is the street made of gold as pure as glass, the walls made of jasper, and the foundation of the city decorated with all manner of precious stones (Rev. 21:18–21).

How do we explain and quantify the love of God for mankind, considering all the provision He made in the garden of Eden before He ever created man in His image and gave dominion power to him to rule over all things? The reconciliation of mankind to Himself was made possible by the sacrifice of His only begotten Son on the cross at Calvary, and the provision of eternal life and His kingdom to accommodate mankind forever.

Beloved, you've known the truth. Live a godly life as if today was your last.

CONCLUSION

Friends, I hope you've been blessed with this Holy Spirit-inspiring, life-GPS book – informative, inspiring, and revealing God's prophetic ordinances over every storms of life.

Having been inspired to write this book, I hereby rededicate my life, my family, and my generation to God the Father, the Son, and the Holy Spirit, and commit the rest of my life to the truth of the gospel. So help me, God. Amen.

Beloved, you're also invited to this Holy Communion table, knowing full well that tomorrow belongs solely to God. Humans only have today. There is wisdom in rededicating our lives to the only faithful and trustworthy God, who can do all things. He is faithful.

TRUST IN THE WORD AND PROMISES OF GOD

'Though its waters roar and foam and the mountains quake with their surging. There is a river whose streams make glad the city of God, the holy place where the Most High dwells' (Ps. 46:3–4).

HYMN FOR THE BOOK

	English		Yoruba – my tongue
1	My hope is built on nothing less Than Jesus Christ, my righteousness; I dare not trust the sweetest frame, But wholly lean on Jesus' name. *On Christ, the solid Rock, I stand.* *All other ground is sinking sand* *All other ground is sinking sand*	1	Igbagbo mi duro lori, Eje at'ododo Jesus, Nko je gbekele ohun kan, Lehin oruko nla Jesu *Mo duro de Kristi Apata)* *Ile miran iyanrin ni) 2ce*
2	When darkness veils His lovely face, I rest on His unchanging grace In every high and stormy gale, My anchor holds within the veil *On Christ, the solid Rock, I stand.* *All other ground is sinking sand* *All other ground is sinking sand.*	2	B'ire ije mi tile gun, Or'ofe re ko yipada B'o ti wu k'iji na le to, Idakoro mi ko ni ye: *Mo dure de Kristi Apata)* *Ile miran iyanrin ni) 2ce*
3		3	Majemu ati eje Re L'emi o romo b'ikun 'mi de Gba ko s'alati lehin mo, O je ireti nla fun mi; *Mo dure de Kristi Apata) Ile miran iyanrin ni) 2ce*
4	His oath, His covenant, His blood, Support me in the whelming flood; When all around my soul gives way, He then is all my hope and stay. *On Christ, the solid Rock, I stand.* *All other ground is sinking sand* *All other ground is sinking sand*	4	'Gbat' ipe kehin ba si dun, A! mba le wa ninu Jesu, Ki nwo ododo re nikan, Ki nduro ni 'waju ite: *Mo dure de Kristi Apata)* *Ile miran iyanrin ni) 2ce* *Amin*
	When He shall come with trumpet sound, Oh, may I then in Him be found; In Him, my righteousness, alone, Faultless to stand before the throne. *On Christ, the solid Rock, I stand.* *All other ground is sinking sand* *All other ground is sinking sand* *Amen*		

OTHER BOOKS

1. GODLY MARRIAGE AND FAMILY LIFE
2. CHRISTIAN MARRIAGE AND FAMILY LIFE

UP COMING BOOKS

1. GOD and HIS KINGDOM LIFE
2. THE GENESIS OF RELIGION
3. HOLY SPIRIT, the abiding GOD
4. VICTORY OF THE CROSS

PRODUCT OF
CHRIST KINGDOM LIFE PUBLICATION AND EVANGELISM
CHRIST KINGDOM (world) OUTREACH MINISERIES

www.christkingdomoutreach.com
email: pastor@christkingdomoutreach.com
Pastorjoy57@gmail.com
Tel: +447950965959

Reaching out to the world with the truth of the Gospel
- Matthew 24:14

ABOUT THE AUTHOR

J. O. Y Aladetan was raised from the despised, from the mud, mire, and slimy pit, to preach the good news of the kingdom of God to all races, tribes, kings, kingdoms, and nations. God set his feet on the mountaintop to cry aloud uncompromisingly to the household of Jacob with the truth of the gospel. By His grace, Joseph sits in the offices of evangelist, pastor, and teacher. He founded Christ Kingdom (World) Outreach Ministries.

www.christkingdomoutreach.com
www.josephaladetanbook.com
Email: pastor@christkingdomoutreach.com
       pastorjoy57@gmail.com
Tel: +447850965959

ABOUT THE BOOK

Many have surrendered to the lies that the Devil tells them while going through challenges. They have given up their destiny and lost focus on eternity as they face the storms of life. Many have cursed themselves, abandoned their vision, and renounced God during their trials of faith, becoming atheists, sorcerers, and occultists, and completely turning away from God.

Is anything too difficult for God to do? No.

Over the Storms of Life was written to inform, to inspire, to bless, and to transform lives and strengthen faith. Faith is called the spiritual horsepower that God has wonderfully and marvellously planted in all human DNA. We can exercise dominion power, like Him and like Jesus Christ, over every storms in our lives.

This book is a revelation of the secret armour of God against every storms that tries to contend with the will of God in human lives. It shows His faithfulness and trustworthiness from eternity past to eternity without end. God will never fail in whatever He wills and promises to do, even when physical circumstances and situations suggest otherwise.

Success begins where failure ends! Failure and tribulation are the ladders to move you to the next level when you activate the spiritual horsepower of faith. Trust God's Word and His covenant promises. Don't settle for the rat race. Strive for God's inheritance.

www.ingramcontent.com/pod-product-compliance
Lightning Source LLC
Chambersburg PA
CBHW020454030426
42337CB00011B/114